NOW OR NEVER

How We Can Save Our Public Schools

NOW OR NEVER

How We Can Save Our Public Schools

By
Tom Luce

With Chris Tucker

TAYLOR PUBLISHING
DALLAS, TEXAS

Published by Taylor Publishing Company
1550 West Mockingbird Lane
Dallas, Texas 75235

Grateful acknowledgment is made to the following
for permission to reprint previously published material:

Designed by: Steve Willgren

Library of Congress Cataloging-in-Publication Data

Luce, Tom.
        Now or never : how we can save our public schools / by Tom Luce,
    with Chris Tucker.
                p.   cm.
        Includes bibliographical references (p. 171) and index.
        ISBN 0-87833-108-5. — ISBN 0-87833-109-3 (pbk.)
        1. Public schools—Texas.   2. Educational change—Texas.
    3. School management and organization—Texas.   I. Tucker, Chris.
    II. Title.
    LA370.L83   1995
    371'.01'09764—dc20   95-8147
                                                                  CIP

Printed in the United States of America

10 9 8 7 6 5 4 3 2 1

CONTENTS

Acknowledgments vi

Introduction 1

CHAPTER 1   A State Still at Risk: Ten Years of Reform—
but the Job Isn't Finished 5

CHAPTER 2   How Bad Are Our Schools? 13

CHAPTER 3   Why We Must Save the Schools—Now 26

CHAPTER 4   Decide on the Results We Want 38

CHAPTER 5   Give Authority to Those Responsible for Results . . . 52

CHAPTER 6   Measure and Reward Results 64

CHAPTER 7   Change What Happens in the Classroom:
Encourage Experimentation, Insist on
Discipline, Teach Virtue. 84

CHAPTER 8   Overhaul Our School Finance System. 100

CHAPTER 9   What You Can Do Now to Save Our Schools 112

Notes. 133

Appendices. 137

Selected Bibliography 171

Index 183

ACKNOWLEDGMENTS

❖

When I first became involved with education reform in 1983, my prior experience consisted of my own public school education and that of two of my children. Everything I have learned since has come from hundreds of dedicated education professionals, parents, students, and taxpayers. I have also read everything I could get my hands on about this important subject.

Having learned so much from so many, it is impossible for me to give individual credit to everyone who has shaped my thinking and strengthened my determination to do something about the condition of our public schools. The Appendix includes the sources of as many facts and figures as possible, as well as much supplemental material, and I have included a bibliography of some of the various books and other publications

I have studied over the years. While I'm grateful to all my teachers, I assume complete responsibility for the conclusions I've reached.

I also want to thank Chris Tucker for his help in producing this book. A former teacher and a perceptive writer, he has helped me to express my thoughts in ways that I hope will expand the public dialogue on this vital issue—and forever cure me of writing in legalese! It was a happy coincidence that he approached me about writing this book at the very time when I had decided to do just that. However, in all fairness to Chris, I must assume responsibility for the views expressed in this book. In addition, a word of thanks to Clark Thomas, a graduate student at the University of Texas at Dallas, who made sure all my facts and figures were correct.

Last, but most important, I want to express my thanks, appreciation, and love to my partner for thirty-five years, my wife Pam, who as always has encouraged me every step of the way.

INTRODUCTION

My thinking about public education in Texas and the future of our state was forever changed by a phone call I received late in the summer of 1983 appointing me Chief of Staff of the Select Committee on Public Education.

I learned a lot about our school system and our state during the next nine crowded months that led to the passage of House Bill 72. I have been involved with public education ever since. During the more than ten years since that fateful call, I have visited public schools and met with people concerned about education all across our huge and diverse state. Everywhere I've gone, from Houston to El Paso to McAllen to Sherman to Odessa and back home to Dallas, I have met with people who have grappled with the daunting problems that face our schools:

• The suburban school principal who was so discouraged because the superintendent kept rejecting any discussion of new programs and higher standards, telling her "Don't rock the boat."

- The principals in Houston who struggle with a student turnover rate of more than two hundred percent caused by parents who move constantly, desperate for a month's free rent.
- The Dallas principal who would not give up trying to help "her kids," many of whom were being abused at home. She rounded up psychiatrists who volunteered their time to help teachers and principals deal with the abuse.
- The African-American principal who set high standards, insisted his low-income students could learn, demanded they learn, and then had to face a year-long investigation by administrators who suspected cheating after his kids did so well on their tests.
- The teachers in the new kindergarten program in Odessa who give of themselves daily in working conditions that would break your heart, for wages that do not begin to reward their dedication and ability.
- The president of one of the largest employers in Dallas, who shared with me his shock and concern when he learned that more than 1,000 of his employees who were losing their present jobs could not qualify for other jobs within the company because they were functionally illiterate.

Some of what I've seen has made me proud of tireless educators, hopeful parents, and bright students. But I've felt my share of anger at teachers and principals who have given up and are merely serving their time. I've been frustrated by elected leaders who talk about the importance of education but are not willing to undertake the political battles to bring about real change.

All of these experiences—the good, bad, and ugly—have

convinced me that we *must* save our public schools and that we *can* save our public schools—but we do not have much time to get the job done. That's why this book is called *Now or Never: How We Can Save Our Public Schools.*

We must act fast because if we do not get this job done soon, increasing public frustration with soaring costs, lack of discipline, and poor academic results will cause taxpayers to lose their dwindling faith in the public schools. Texans will give up on their schools and salve their consciences by demanding a voucher system. This will help a few students but will doom millions of our public school children to lives of unfulfilled potential, saddling our state with a second-rate economy and a lower standard of living. (It will also ruin private schools—but more about that later.)

For so many reasons, we can't let that happen. Besides the many "public-minded" reasons for fighting to save our schools, I have personal reasons as well. Like so many other Texans, I owe an everlasting debt to an educator—my third-grade teacher, Mrs. Brooks, who awakened me to the value of education and thus enabled me to live the American dream. And my grandson John is a first-grader at Robert E. Lee Elementary School in Austin, where I hope he'll find his own Mrs. Brooks. Four more grandsons will start the first grade in the near future.

But saving the schools, for my grandchildren and for all the children of Texas, will take more than small, incremental changes to our system of education. Tinkering around the edges is not enough because the problem is not just on the edges. As we'll see, our current system needs to be radically transformed into something new and vital, something that resembles the current system no more than modern medicine resembles the crude practices of the Middle Ages.

The main purpose of this book is twofold: First, to unite parents, educators, taxpayers, business people, all of us, in a dramatic, radical reshaping of our public schools. Second, to set out a practical, step-by-step program for accomplishing that mission.

I believe we can do no less because our kids deserve no less than excellent public schools. But before we talk about a better future for our schools, let's look back for a brief history of recent school reform efforts in Texas.

CHAPTER I

A STATE STILL AT RISK

Ten Years of Reform—but the Job Isn't Finished

Americans are a proud people, and with good reason. Militarily and economically, we've long been the leader of the world. But some of our confidence began eroding in 1983 with the publication of a report called *A Nation at Risk*. Compiled by the National Commission on Excellence in Education, the report contained irrefutable evidence that our public schools were failing in their basic mission to educate our young people.

Page after page showed that by almost every measure, we were slipping behind other industrialized countries. Like fingernails raking down a chalkboard, *A Nation at Risk* got the nation's attention with some alarming criticism.

If an unfriendly foreign power had attempted to impose on America the mediocre educational performance that exists today, we might well have viewed it as an act of war. As it stands, we have allowed this to happen to ourselves…we have, in effect, been committing an act of unthinking, unilateral educational disarmament.[1]

As the shock waves ran through the country, Texas became the first state to counterattack, launching a major education reform effort—albeit by political accident.

In 1983, the Texas Legislature failed to pass Governor Mark White's campaign promise of an across-the-board pay increase for Texas teachers. To save political face for Governor White, the Legislature and the Governor agreed to create a statewide commission to examine the teacher pay issue and to study how our education system could be improved. Many expected the commission to rubber-stamp a pay increase for teachers, issue some platitudes about the glories of education, and quietly fold its tents, but the commission took seriously its sweeping mandate. The result was House Bill 72, the most comprehensive school reform effort of the eighties. States such as South Carolina, led by then-Governor Richard Riley (now Secretary of Education); Tennessee, led by then-Governor and later Secretary of Education Lamar Alexander; and Arkansas, led by then-Governor Bill Clinton, followed Texas's lead in many respects. Virtually every state in the union passed reform bills, but no effort was more ambitious and sweeping than that of Texas. (See Appendix, page 138.)

Among many other accomplishments, House Bill 72

- **Raised student performance standards.** A passing grade was raised from a sixty to a seventy; the now-famous "no pass, no play" rule limited participation in extracurricular activities to students who were passing their courses; students could miss no more than five class days and still get credit for a course.
- **Raised school standards.** Schools were required to offer pre-kindergarten and summer programs for at-risk students

and students with limited English proficiency. The bill also required that extracurricular activities be conducted before or after school, not during the school day. Schools were required to reduce class sizes in grades kindergarten through fourth to no more than twenty-two students per teacher.

- **Insisted upon assessment.** Students were required to pass a statewide test to get a diploma; and statewide tests were required in reading, writing, and math for all students in grades one, three, five, seven, and nine.
- **Addressed the issue of teacher quality.** The teacher career ladder was established to provide bonuses to teachers who were rated highly in appraisals; the bill also mandated more in-service training time for teachers and established a one-time test to weed out incompetent teachers.
- **Increased funding for both poor and rich school districts.**

It's no exaggeration to say that House Bill 72 saved a patient who was slipping into a coma. Declining test scores were arrested, and we sent a strong message that the state would require at least minimum standards.

Most of the provisions have worked as planned. Despite continual moaning from coaches who claim "some boys can't learn" and warn that youngsters will turn to crime if they can't play football, the "no pass, no play" provision stands as a constant reminder that schoolwork comes first. The requirement that all students take a battery of statewide tests has given Texans the hard data—the test scores—with which to judge how well the schools are doing. (The howls of protest from some professional educators are proof enough that assessment is having the desired effect.) Smaller class sizes are giving younger students, particularly the at-risk students, a chance to receive the foundation they need to succeed in middle school and high school.

The statewide test for teachers also helped, even though the

Texas Education Agency watered it down to an eleventh-grade literacy test and, outrageously, teachers were given two tries to pass it! Even with the bar set that low, more than five thousand teachers either flunked the test twice or refused to take the test and were removed from the classroom.

Not every idea in House Bill 72 worked as we had hoped. For example, the education bureaucracy, which favors lockstep rewards for all teachers regardless of merit, (see Chapter 7) managed to neutralize the teacher career ladder by rating virtually every teacher as "outstanding" and then complaining that there was not enough money to give every one of these "outstanding" teachers a bonus.

WHO THWARTED CHANGE? MEET THE IRON TRIANGLE

And so you're wondering: Well, after all that work, why aren't our schools perfect, or at least very, very good? Why do we still have high dropout rates, especially among minorities? Why do we have so many students unable to solve problems in algebra or write a coherent paragraph? The answer to that is threefold.

First, the system is huge. It's hard enough to change the culture of a small, privately held company. It's tremendously hard to transform an institution the size and scale of the Texas public schools. Remember, the ten largest private sector employers in Texas combined—including General Motors, Halliburton Company, Texas Instruments, AMR Corporation, and Wal-Mart—have 100,000 fewer workers than the Texas public school system, which employed 434,024 people during the 1993–1994 school year.[2]

Second, House Bill 72 was intended to be part of a process, not an end in itself. When we presented our recommendations to the Legislature, we told lawmakers over and over that House Bill 72 was only the first step in a long march to transform our schools. Only so much reform can be assimilated at one time. Our intention was that subsequent legislatures would build on our efforts.

There have been other incremental reforms, but for the past several years the Legislature has spent most of its energy and time arguing about funding—"Robin Hood" and "Son of Robin Hood"—instead of trying to change what happens in the classroom. (In Chapter 8, we'll discuss the futility of changing the funding mechanism without revamping the entire system.)

Third, what I call the Iron Triangle continues its entrenched opposition to a radical overhaul of the schools. The Iron Triangle, of course, consists of the Texas Education Agency, the Legislature, and the innumerable education associations that populate Austin. It's worth getting to know these players, because any future reform effort is going to run smack into the same heavyweights.

The Texas Education Agency (TEA) is a typical government agency that too often has been more concerned with centralized control of the "process" of education rather than the "output" or results of education. In addition, TEA is overly sensitive to Austin politics and insensitive to its true customers—students and parents.

That's just fine with the Legislature, which prefers that the TEA, the education associations, and legislative staff, working together, write most education legislation or at least "sign off" on the bills.

And then we have the associations, more than one hundred of them, representing every conceivable interest group–coaches, teachers, vocational education teachers, school nurses, guidance counselors, and more. (See Appendix, page 139.) I'd be surprised if there is not an Association of Coaches Who Used to Be Principals and Then Went Back to Coaching. With a few notable exceptions, these associations consider it their sacred duty to get all their members a pay raise, protect everyone's job, and preserve the status quo in the schoolhouse.

Back in 1984, I learned just how closely the members of the Iron Triangle cooperate. When I would describe one of our recommendations to a legislator, his or her first words would not be a comment or question about the substance of the provision, but an inquiry: Did I know how a particular teacher's group or the Superintendents Association or the School Board Association or some other group felt about the provision? That was what pushed the legislator's buttons—not the worth of the proposal, but how it would play with the Iron Triangle.

Historically, major education bills were worked out in the back rooms, in meetings with the associations and legislative staff. All of that changed temporarily in 1984, when the Select Committee was able to mobilize the business community and the editorial boards of major newspapers across the state in support of change. Together, business and the media put pressure on the legislature to pass House Bill 72. We were also able to form a coalition with Ernie Cortes and the Industrial Areas Foundation, a grass roots organization that works on issues important to low-income people, such as education and health care. As we came to see, it was a good thing we had allies like Ernie.

Thanks to these efforts, for the first time the power of the Iron Triangle was blunted. The general public was brought into the back rooms, demanding to be heard on behalf of the kids. Because of this outcry, we passed the most substantive changes in education policy in many years, despite the opposition of most education associations.

(There were two notable exceptions who broke ranks with the Iron Triangle. We got support from the Texas Elementary Principals and Supervisors Association, who recognized the importance of smaller classes in grades kindergarten through fourth and the pre-kindergarten programs; and the Texas Federation of Teachers, the state affiliate of the American Federation of Teachers led by Albert Shanker.)

Despite the efforts of these courageous educators, the business community, the public at large, major newspapers, and citizen reformers like Ernie Cortes, we almost lost the battle to the guardians of the status quo.

The darkest moment was the night of the Father's Day Massacre, so named because on Father's Day in June, 1984, the House Education Committee gutted House Bill 72. It appeared that we had lost the battle that night. We were running out of time in the special session and it looked like we would not even get our bill to the floor of the house for a vote.

The day was saved when, the next morning, Ernie Cortes arranged for twelve busloads of people to take off from work and come to Austin from San Antonio. These dedicated citizens walked the halls of the capitol, exhorting legislators to reverse themselves and vote on House Bill 72. For the first time, some legislators realized that the public at large was demanding to be heard as well as the special interests. Within two weeks, House Bill 72 became law. School reform had taken its first steps in Texas.

I'm proud of my role in stabilizing the patient. I shudder to think where our schools might be right now if House Bill 72 had gone down in flames. But I'm the first to tell you that House Bill 72 did not go far enough. After all that effort and all that money, our schools have gone from a grade of F to a C—and a C will not be a passing grade in the increasingly competitive, worldwide economy of the Information Age.

That's because, as revolutionary as it might have seemed in the mid-eighties, House Bill 72 was really marginal, incremental reform—tinkering at the edges of the problem. It was as if we tried to revive the Pony Express by using faster horses and lighter saddles instead of preparing for the future—the telegraph, the airplane, the Internet. House Bill 72 was an attempt to make evolutionary change to a system that was no longer in touch with the culture or the workplace.

What we must now realize is that the Pony Express is gone forever. The next wave of school reform in Texas must go beyond *evolutionary* change to *revolutionary* change. Only a change of that magnitude will be enough to reverse the heartbreaking decline of our schools.

CHAPTER 2

HOW BAD ARE OUR SCHOOLS?

It wouldn't be fair or accurate to say there is no good news about our schools. There is good news. Every indicator of student performance for the past three years shows that student achievement is up.

In 1994, the results of the statewide Texas Assessment of Academic Skills (TAAS) showed improvement over the 1993 scores, with higher scores in every group tested. Minorities and the economically disadvantaged posted gains along with white students, doing especially well on the fourth-grade level.[1] Student performance on the TAAS tests over the past three years is likewise up in every category.

TAAS 1994 Results

All Tests Taken–4th Grade

	Spring 1993 (Spring '94 Standard)	Spring 1994	Difference
All	46%	54%	+8
African American	26%	33%	+7
Hispanic	32%	43%	+11
White	61%	66%	+5
Economically Disadvantaged	31%	40%	+9

All Tests Taken–8th Grade

	Spring 1993 (Spring '94 Standard)	Spring 1994	Difference
All	45%	49%	+4
African American	22%	27%	+5
Hispanic	27%	33%	+6
White	62%	65%	+3
Economically Disadvantaged	25%	31%	+6

All Tests Taken–10th Grade

	Spring 1993 (Spring '94 Standard)	Spring 1994	Difference
All	51%	52%	+1
African American	29%	29%	0
Hispanic	34%	35%	+1
White	66%	67%	+1
Economically Disadvantaged	31%	33%	+2

Student Performance–3 Year Trends
TAAS Tests, Grades 4, 8 and 10

All Tests Taken–4th Grade

All	+10
African American	+7
Hispanic	+12
White	+8
Economically Disadvantaged	+11

All Tests Taken–8th Grade

All	+8
African American	+6
Hispanic	+7
White	+8
Economically Disadvantaged	+9

All Tests Taken–10th Grade

All	+3
African American	+1
Hispanic	+2
White	+5
Economically Disadvantaged	+3

Source: Texas Education Agency

And there's more good news: dropout rates are lower and have been falling for three years. SAT, ACT and PSAT test scores are also up.[2] (See Appendix, pages 140–141.)

The best news, in my mind, is that students statewide are taking more core academic courses than ever before—more algebra, more physics, more geography. (See Appendix, page 142.) This trend will inevitably result in higher levels of student achievement.

But these TAAS scores and other indicators, though welcome, are really just flickering candles in a dark night. If we look at these numbers and conclude that all is well, we are kidding ourselves and robbing our kids of the truth. An alcoholic can't get well until he admits there's a problem, and we can't create a vital new school system until we take a long, sober look at the bad news about our schools.

These rising TAAS scores must be seen in the context of a school system that demands far too little of our students. It works like this:

Suppose I tell you that I have just set a new personal best as a high jumper. You smile, shake my hand, and ask how high I've jumped.

"Three feet," I say, grinning from ear to ear.

You're puzzled. Three feet?

"Uh, well, that's not very high," you say. "Almost anyone can clear three feet."

"True," I say. "But last year, I was clearing only two feet. I've made a fifty percent gain in just one year!"

Our kids are jumping higher lately, but the bar is set too low. To put the TAAS gains in perspective, consider that the Texas Education Agency recently released its 1994 Accountability Ratings of more than six thousand school campuses in our state. The rating system is complex (See Appendix, page 143), but in essence the grading standards were as follows:

- Exemplary: At least ninety percent of a school's students passing all three TAAS subject area tests—reading, writing, and mathematics.
- Recognized: At least sixty-five percent passing each subject area test.
- Accredited/Acceptable: More than twenty-five percent passing each subject area test.
- Accredited Warned/Low Performing: Less than twenty-five percent passing any subject area.

The results were:

1993-1994 CAMPUS RATING

	1993	1994	
Exemplary	22	66	
Recognized	256	517	
Acceptable	5580	5171	
Low Performing	326	57	
Delayed		2	
Not Rated		276	(early childhood/kindergarten)
Pending		254	(alternative education requests)
Total	6184	6343	

You'll notice that more than eighty percent of our campuses are rated "acceptable," a term which borders on deceptive advertising. That means that many of our schools may have as few as twenty-six percent of their students passing the statewide achievement tests in reading, writing, and mathematics. Flip that over, and you see the bad news: At many of these schools, as many as seventy-four percent of students *cannot* pass all the tests.[3]

In fact, a close look at the 1994 TAAS scores reveals clearly, notwithstanding the progress we have made, how far we have to go.

The bottom line is this:

Forty-six percent of all 4th-graders did not pass all sections of the TAAS test.
Fifty-one percent of 8th graders did not pass all sections of the TAAS test.
Forty-eight percent of 10th graders did not pass all sections of the TAAS test.

It's also clear that we have miles to go in educating minority students. In the fourth grade, fifty-seven percent of all Hispanic students failed at least one TAAS test; sixty-seven percent in the eighth grade failed at least one; and in the tenth grade, sixty-five percent failed at least one.[4] Failure to improve Hispanic education will result in economic disaster in the years to come, as Hispanics will become the state's largest ethnic or racial group sometime around the year 2020.

Given these test scores, it should come as no surprise that nearly thirty percent of Texas college freshmen recently failed a state academic skills test, the Texas Academic Skills Program. Those who fail the TASP test must take remedial classes and cannot take junior level courses in a four-year college or graduate from community college until they pass the test. As a result, Texas spends $65 million each year on remedial courses in our colleges and universities.[5]

It's bad enough when massive numbers of failures are rated "acceptable," but there's worse news in those figures: Only sixty-six campuses out of 6,343—*less than one percent of our schools*—are rated "exemplary," meaning that ninety percent or more of the students passed all three tests. If you're in search of real excellence in Texas schools, you had better pack your lunch and wear your walking shoes, because you'll be searching a long time. And we could easily be looking at worse numbers than these; the Commissioner of Education had proposed tougher criteria for the first campus rankings but abandoned the notion after squawks of protest from the education community. As we seek to compete in the global economy of the twenty-first century, "acceptable" will not get the job done. We need much more "exemplary" work from our students.

THE HARD FACTS: TEXAS VERSUS AMERICA

It's not enough to compare Texas kids against each other. Eventually, our kids will compete with graduates from Florida, California, New York, and all the other states. Our state already competes with other states for corporate relocations, which often depend in part on the quality of the schools.

Sadly, we don't have much room for those Texas brags when you match our educational performance against that of other states. We continue to rank in the lower tier:

- Forty-first out of fifty states on the 1994 Scholastic Aptitude Test, with an average score of 886.
- Fourteenth out of the twenty-three states in which the SAT is more widely taken. (For example, only five percent of students in Iowa took the SAT while forty-nine percent of Texas high school graduates took the test in 1991-92.)
- Forty-seventh out of fifty states in adult literacy. More than six million adult Texans—or *half of the adult population*—cannot calculate a sale price in an ad or read a bus schedule or write a letter explaining a charge account error.[6]
- Fiftieth out of fifty states in public school graduation rate. Between the ninth grade and graduation day, we have a higher percentage of dropouts than any other state.

In short, we don't stack up well against our rival states—and it's not as if those other states have found the magic key to educational excellence. Discussing state rankings, Chester Finn, a former official in the U.S. Department of Education and author of *We Must Take Charge: Our Schools and Our Future*, put it this way to *Newsweek*: "Don't let the fascination with 'which state did better than which state,' blind you to the state of the forest. The forest did dismally."

Nowhere is the dismal state of America's public education better demonstrated than in the results of the National Assessment of Education Progress tests (NAEP), the most comprehensive testing program we have.

- Only twenty-five percent of all students tested could write a well-developed persuasive essay. Even when given fifty minutes to organize and write a response to a statement suggesting that drivers' licenses should be revoked for students with failing grades, only three percent of the twelfth-grade essays were rated as "elaborated" or better. The remainder were rated as "undeveloped," "minimally developed," or simply "developed."
- Only one percent of twelfth-graders can write a satisfactory paragraph summarizing the material in a newspaper *sports* article.
- On NAEP mathematics questions asking students to solve a problem requiring some depth of understanding and to write an explanation of their solution, almost two-thirds provided incorrect answers, indicating little evidence of understanding the mathematics concepts or even the questions being asked. As many as one-fifth of the students left their papers blank. Even students who seemed to understand the questions had difficulty explaining their work.
- Only fifty-nine percent of eighth graders could calculate how many days a person would have to work at two dollars per day for three days a week and three dollars per day for

three other days a week to earn forty-five dollars. Only twenty-two percent of fourth-graders could perform the same calculation.

- Only thirty-five percent of eighth-graders could use a ruler/protractor to find the degree measure of an angle.
- Only twenty-one percent of fourth-graders could use a calculator to compute the change they would receive from a $10.00 bill after a purchase of two items costing $3.92 each.
- Only six percent of twelfth-graders could satisfactorily calculate a tax rate on income above ten thousand dollars and only two percent could calculate the income on which an effective tax rate would be five percent.
- Only six percent of twelfth-graders are able to understand and use the mathematical reasoning and problem-solving skills associated with algebra, geometry, and fractions that prepare them for college level math.

NAEP math tests revealed that fewer than one out of five students in grades 4, 8, and 12 has reached the National Education Goal of demonstrating competency in mathematics.[7] (See chart, page 21.)

In Texas in 1990 only thirteen percent of our eighth graders demonstrated competency in math. Forty-eight percent of our students scored at "below basic" levels.

The scorecard in civics nationwide is not much better. Nearly all twelfth-graders had a basic knowledge of civics, spanning such topics as elections, laws, and constitutional rights. However, only about half understood specific government structures and functions such as separation of powers, and only six percent had a detailed knowledge of the basic institutions of government such as the cabinet and the judiciary.

The level of literacy achievement revealed that while most

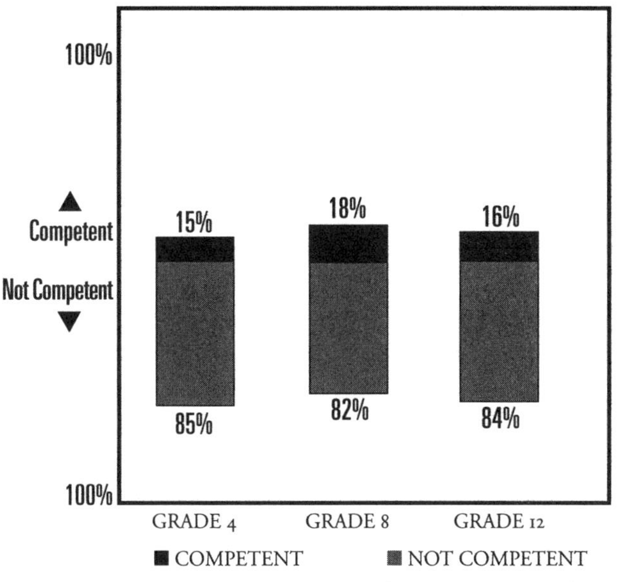

Competency in Mathematics
Percentage of 4th, 8th, and 12th graders who
are competent in mathematics, 1990.

Source: National Assessment Governing Board, 1991

young Americans have mastered the most basic functional literacy skills, few are able to perform more complex literacy tasks requiring them to process and summarize many pieces of information. Because writing and reading are so intimately linked, it comes as no surprise to see that large numbers of our students cannot read at grade level.

The emphasis on achieving minimum skills—the skills measured in the TAAS tests cited on page 14—has clearly resulted in public schools turning out students that cannot meet the increasing skill level demanded by today's employers.

A 1991 Texas Research League survey of businesses revealed that Texas business was "very concerned" about the ability of the state's public school system to prepare a future work force for the state. Forty-three percent of employers contacted had difficulty finding entry-level workers with basic reading, writing, communication, and math skills.[8]

Texas is expected to gain almost 1.4 million jobs by the year 2000, with thirty percent of them requiring a college degree and another twenty-two percent requiring some post-secondary training. High school dropouts will qualify for only fourteen percent of the jobs.

Of the twenty occupations with the largest projected future growth, only eleven require no more than a high school education. These include such jobs as janitor, gardener, and truck driver. Many of the so-called blue collar jobs require computer skills along with reading, writing, and math.[9]

In light of that, it's indefensible that the Texas high school exit test is designed to measure reading and math skills at the tenth-grade level even though many manufacturing jobs require twelfth-grade reading skills to ensure that workers can master technical, quality, and safety manuals.

The National Commission on Children, in its final report in 1991, summed up our country's educational shortcomings this way:

> In recent national assessments, American students performed poorly on reading, mathematics, science and writing tests. Fewer than half of American 17-year-olds who are in school possess the skills and basic knowledge required for college and many entry-level jobs. Similarly, fewer than half can understand complicated literacy and information passages that are typical of high school work or can evaluate the results or procedures of a scientific study. Only 59 percent can compute with decimals, fractions and percentages or solve simple equations. Many are so limited in their command of written English that they are unable to communicate in a reasoned point of view.[10]

MORE HARD FACTS: TEXAS VERSUS THE WORLD

When you compare American students to their counterparts in other countries—our foreign competitors—the picture is equally bleak. For several years running, American students have scored poorly on International Assessment of Educational Progress exams in science and math, outperformed by, among others, Korea, Spain, the United Kingdom, Canada, Hungary, and Ireland. As the chart below shows, our position is embarrassing indeed.

Achievement in Mathematics

Average percent correct on mathematics items from the
International Assessment of Educational Progress (IAEP), 1991.

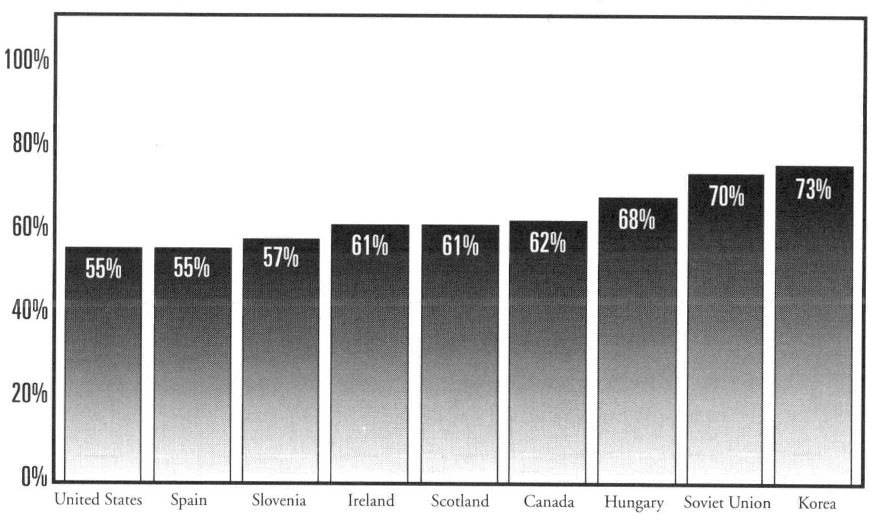

Source: Educational Testing Service, 1992

In one of the most depressing reports of all, the National Commission on Children summarized our international performance as follows:

Assessments of 20 school systems around the world rank American eighth-graders 10th in arithmetic, 12th in algebra and 16th in geometry. Even America's top students fare poorly in international comparisons: Among the

Achievement in Science
Average percent correct on mathematics items from the
International Assessment of Educational Progress (IAEP), 1991.

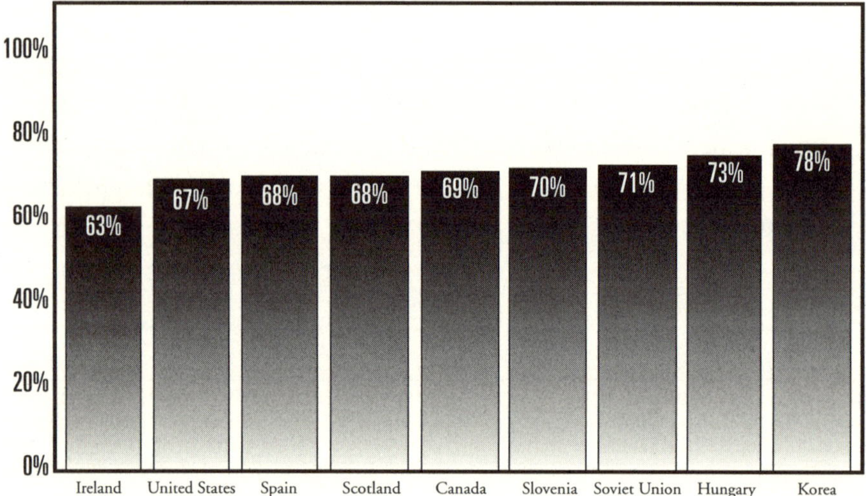

Source: Educational Testing Service, 1992

top one percent of high school seniors, American students ranked last. Achievement in science is no better. Among 10-year olds in 15 countries, Americans rank eighth. Among 14-year olds in 17 countries, Americans tie with children in Singapore and Thailand for 14th place. Among advanced science students in 12 nations, Americans are eleventh in chemistry, ninth in physics and last in biology.[11]

This summary dramatically presents a seldom noted point: We are also failing at the *top* of the academic pyramid. Too often we focus only on the failures of our school system at the bottom of the pyramid.

Recently the American Federation of Teachers conducted a comprehensive review of actual examinations taken by students seeking college entrance in England, Wales, Germany, France, and Japan, and compared them with the U.S. Advanced Placement biology exam. The results are depressing. From thirty to nearly sixty percent of students in England, Wales, France, Germany, and Japan take advanced biology exams and twenty-five to thirty-six percent pass them. In the United States only seven percent of students even take the Advanced Placement biology exam. Only four percent score three or better—the equivalent of passing.

AFT president Albert Shanker explains the disparity this way: "How did they manage?" he says of the foreign education systems. "They did it the hard way—by maintaining their high standards and telling kids, 'if you want to go to college, you must learn this material and pass these exams.' We tell students, 'we will help you.'"[12] Too often, in too many schools, we allow students to get away with doing the minimum.

When it comes to the schools, our nation and our state are still at risk. But despite all the problems that beset them, our schools can and must be saved. Here's why.

WHY WE MUST SAVE THE SCHOOLS—NOW

"No man is an island, entire unto himself," said John Donne in a famous meditation about the things that bind us together. We are not islands, self-sufficient units. We're connected to each other, whether we realize it or not, in communities large and small.

Today in Texas we are in danger of losing one of the great builders and preservers of community: our public school system. Ask not for whom the bell tolls. It tolls for the schools, unless we act now.

Maybe you don't have kids, or your kids are grown, or they go to private schools. Maybe you think the schools have declined so far and failed so completely that they are not worth saving. But public schools are vital to your future whatever your individual circumstances. And they can be saved. They *must* be saved, because the future of our state is inextricably tied to the future of our schools. Consider:

• If you are concerned about crime—and who isn't?—remember that eighty-five percent of Texas prison inmates are high school dropouts. Forty-five percent of inmates are illiterate or read below the sixth grade level. It costs us about $13,000 a year to house each inmate, and much more if the prisoner has health problems.[1] By contrast, we spend about $5,000 a year to educate a child who stays in school.[2]

Which seems like the better deal to you? Of course some of the people who go to prison are incorrigible troublemakers, bad seeds. But we have to hope that many inmates might have taken another road in life had they possessed the education and job skills to make a decent living on the right side of the law. We can pay now for quality education, or pay later for dead-end warehousing of people who contribute little beyond crime and violence.

Perhaps you are saying to yourself, "Well, I'll just insulate my family from all this. I'll move off to some nice walled community in a prosperous, homogeneous suburb or put my kids in private school."

Good luck. Unfortunately, you'll be paying both public school taxes that continue to rise every year *and* private school tuition. And if your kids do get that wonderful private school education and someday own their own business, where will they find qualified employees? How will their business compete in a worldwide economy if United States students continue to rank at or near the bottom on most international tests? How will you shield your families from drive-by shootings and other random, violent crimes that plague both suburbs and inner cities?

Again, there are no islands where we can hide from the problems of our schools. Our future, and our children's future, is tied to the success of our schools.

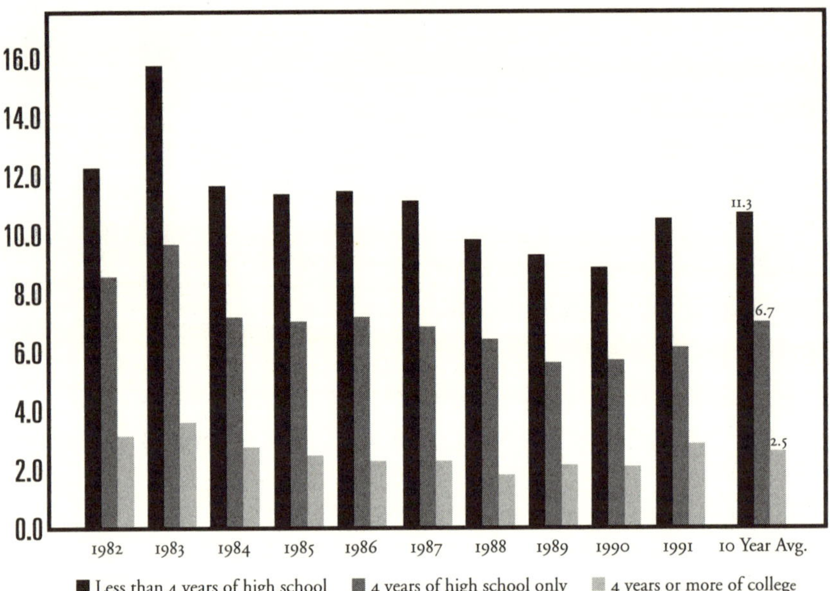

**Unemployment Rate by Educational Attainment
1982-1991**

Source: U.S. Bureau of the Census, Statistical Abstract of the United States: 1992
(112th Edition) Washington, DC, 1992

• If you're concerned about job creation, keep in mind that our state's economy has undergone a radical and permanent shift. In the "good old days" that lasted up until the 1970s in Texas, a hard-working young man could drop out of school, go to work in the oil fields or on the farm, and make enough to buy a home, provide for his family, and retire to a nice life of fishing.

Those days are gone forever. Oil and gas will never again be the mainstays of the Texas economy. The auto mechanic of today must be computer literate, be able to read complex manuals, know how to solve problems and work in teams.

Sadly, our schools have not kept pace with the changing economy. For years one of the largest employers in the Dallas–Fort Worth area, a high-tech company with an international reputation, went out of state to hire entry-level people because management could not find enough high school graduates with a sufficient degree of literacy to fill those jobs. These high-tech, entry-level jobs are the equivalent of the auto assembly-line jobs of the past. In the Information Age, lack of education means unemployment.

• If you're concerned with the rising tax burden you bear—and who isn't?—think what your tax bill will be in ten years if half our state's population lacks the skills to hold a decent job. The failure rate on the Texas Assessment of Academic Skills test is close to fifty percent. Among minorities, it's about seventy percent—and in the 1990s, minorities became the majority in Texas public schools.

If you worry about soaring welfare costs and unemployment in our state, understand this truth of the 1990s: "The more you learn, the more you earn." There's a definite correlation between years of education and earning power. Education turns tax *spenders* into tax*payers.*

The U.S. Census Bureau reported the following lifetime earnings for people who achieve various levels of education:[3]

No high school diploma	$ 609,000
High school diploma	821,000
Some college	993,000
Associate's Degree	1,062,000
Bachelor's Degree	1,421,000
Master's Degree	1,619,000
Doctorate	2,142,000
Professional	3,013,000

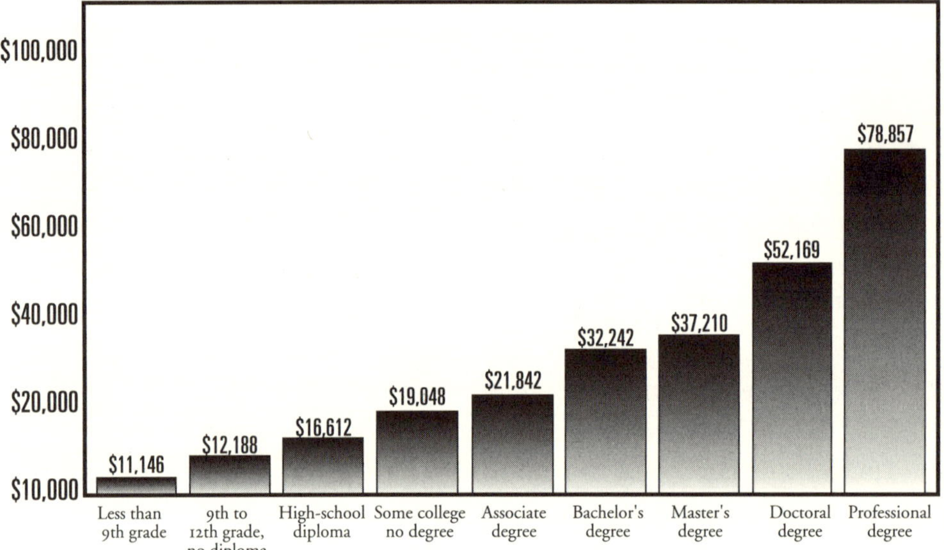

So there is a strong economic argument for saving our public schools. But man does not live by bread alone. The schools do much more than create workers and taxpayers; they also train responsible citizens.

> If a nation expects to be ignorant and free, in a state of civilization, it expects what never was and never will be.—Thomas Jefferson[4]

Education and citizenship are linked in at least two ways. First, our schools must be the guardians of our democratic heritage. The schools must remind each new generation that America was born out of a struggle for freedom and that our country is dedicated to principles such as free speech, equal justice, and fair representation—the privileges of freedom.

But the schools must also prepare citizens for the *responsibilities* of freedom. Because a democratic government answers to the will of the people, the people must have the reading, writing, and reasoning skills required to carry out those responsibilities. The young man who can barely read the daily newspaper isn't going to be much help when it comes to electing qualified leaders. The young woman who doesn't understand the workings of a market economy or the judicial system is likely to feel alienated when it comes time to cast a vote.

Our Texas schools are charged with educating some 3.6 million youngsters each year. If our public schools fail in their mission, we'll raise a generation that knows and cares little about the privileges and responsibilities of freedom. Our public schools reflect the health of our society; declining schools both cause and reflect a decline in citizenship.

The public schools can also help us learn to live and work together in an increasingly diverse society. With no military draft, the schools are one of the few places where people of different races and social classes can learn to work together. We talk a lot about diversity today, but we need unity as well, lest we break up into Balkanized factions glaring and snarling at each other across cultural barriers. The schools can teach respect for diversity while providing the cultural "glue" that will hold us together.

Beyond the economic and cultural arguments for saving our schools, there are the reasons we see in our children's eyes when we put them to bed at night. We have a moral duty to treat each child as a priceless gift from God, a small package of hopes and dreams and potential unlike any other. There is no better way to "love thy neighbor" than by helping to create schools in which all our children can flourish and realize their potential. When we do our best for the kids, we are doing God's work on earth.

In short, we cannot run or hide from the problem. We must stand and fight for our schools. Your future, the future of Texas, and the future of America are at stake.

The time is right to fix our schools and they can be fixed. Believe me, I know it will not be easy. It will be slow—like turning the *Queen Mary*. But it can be done and now is the time.

Why do I believe we can do this job? And why now? For several reasons.

First, the public is aware of the problem and is beginning to demand that it be fixed. In a democracy, radical change cannot be forced on people from the top down. It must come from the bottom up, from the people themselves. Whether it's the success of Mothers Against Drunk Driving, the recycling movement, or the national trend against smoking in public places, true change comes when large numbers of people decide that the status quo is no longer tolerable.

When we started working on education reform in 1983, the vast majority of people in Texas were unaware of the magnitude of the problem. So our first task was to lay the groundwork for reform. We had to convince Texans that we had a problem.

Today we don't have to spend time convincing Texans that the dike is full of holes and we're running out of thumbs. They know it. If anything, we have the opposite problem: Too many people believe the problems of the schools are insurmountable.

That's why it's vital that we act now. I've talked to so many Texans over the past few years who don't want to write off the schools. They want to save them—and we can do it if we put our minds and hearts into the task. We've learned a lot since the days of House Bill 72. We know what works and what does not work. We've made progress and we know how to make more. Since our effort, virtually every state has taken steps to improve its schools. We can draw on their examples as well.

Second, the reform movement has brought allies together. Like guerrilla fighters who feared their cause was lost, these diehards have come out of hiding to discover they are not alone. Many longtime educators feel understandably threatened by the rise of the voucher movement, and they're refusing to give up on the promise of public schools. These range from history teachers in small Texas towns to Albert Shanker, president of the American Federation of Teachers, who has told his members since 1988 that they must support a revolution in the way we educate our young people or they would face extinction, just as the American automobile worker was facing extinction before the automobile industry finally faced reality and began restructuring.

Third, more and more Texas parents are coming to agree with management expert Peter Drucker, who made this forecast about what he calls the emerging knowledge society:

> ...the performance of the schools and the basic values of the schools will be of increasing concern to society as a whole, rather than being considered professional matters that can safely be left to 'educators.'[5]

Driven by a number of forces—exploding property taxes, concern over values, civic pride—parents are getting involved in the schools, supporting the best teachers, and demanding more of them.

And when these parents want hard facts about the schools, they can get them because the reform movement forced assessment and accountability onto the table, despite the resistance of the education establishment. Where once a parent had to rely on word of mouth to separate the successful schools from the failing schools, now the test scores are out there in the light of day. The reform movement has given citizens the facts and figures they need to challenge the education lobbies. That increases the pressure to change.

Fourth, and perhaps most encouraging, reinforcements are on the way. In the eighties it seemed that every capable youngster wanted to go to law school or business school, or become Bob Woodward. The reform movement has encouraged a new generation of bright, caring individuals to go into education. Now if we can give them the salaries they deserve…but let's not get ahead of ourselves.

As we've seen, Texas schools in the eighties were like a critically ill patient who was sinking fast. House Bill 72 stabilized the patient by putting minimal standards in place. The bleeding was stopped. SAT scores, which had been on a steady decline before the reform movement, took wing in the mid-eighties, have risen slightly. But we can't stop now! "Test scores are up five points!" is no battle cry for the future. The pressure is building for real change. Now we must go beyond minimum standards and strive for excellence.

Earlier I spoke of a revolution to transform our schools. In the rest of this book, we're going to outline the stages of that transformation.

That transformation must start with a commitment by everyone involved—principals, teachers, parents—that every child can learn: rich, poor, black, white, Hispanic. Lip service will not suffice. We must act upon the conviction that every child is a unique gift from God. Our goal must be to help all children get the education that will help them fulfill their potential and fully utilize their unique bundle of talents.

As we move toward that goal, we've got to be mindful of several considerations: First, academic research confirms that every child learns in a different way and at a different pace. This research must be kept in focus when we consider what changes we need to make to improve our schools. This is particularly true when we consider what policy changes are needed at the state level.

Second, the Texas public school system is huge and diverse. Texas public schools (kindergarten through twelfth grade) budgeted about nineteen billion dollars for the 1993–94 school year.[1] The revenues of the Texas public schools were more than the revenues of EDS and Texas Instruments combined. The only publicly held Texas corporations that had more revenue in 1993 were Exxon and J. C. Penney.[2]

Third, each year, some 3.6 million students pour into our more than six thousand campuses. We have 1,044 school districts ranging in size from almost 200,000 students in Houston to Alanreed's nine students. We employ 226,193 classroom teachers and there were a total of 434,024 public school employees in the 1993–94 school year. In more than half the counties in Texas, the school district is the largest employer.[3]

Fourth, non-Anglo students outnumber Anglo students statewide and will continue to increase dramatically. It is projected that by 2025, Hispanic students will comprise forty-seven percent of the student population.[4]

Given the vast size and complexity of the public school system, there is no silver bullet and no easy fix available. We must have systemic change that takes into account the myriad forces that act upon the system, as illustrated by this diagram.

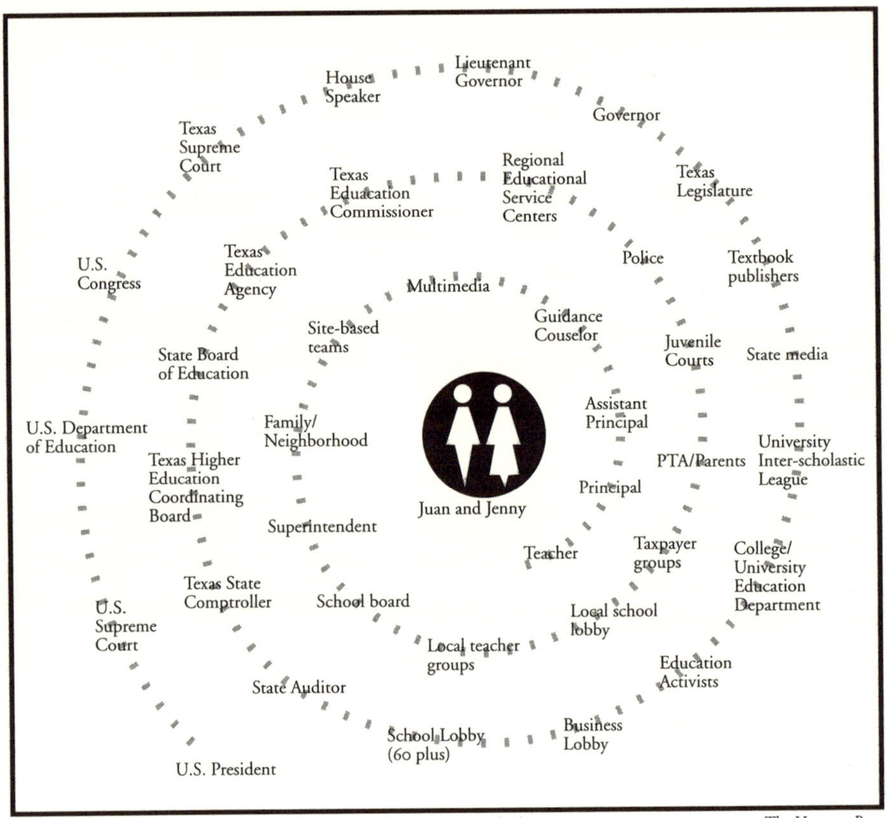

Source: Texas Education Agency; A Houston Post survey asking government leaders, educators and private citizens with a history of involvement in the public school system to comment on how it does or does not work.

The Houston Post

SOLUTIONS

Serious, thorough reforms must ensure that teachers have the flexibility to fine-tune and tailor their instruction to suit the varying needs of this diverse school population. One size does not fit all. But whatever the size of the school district, however diverse the student population, there are certain principles that must be followed if we are to create the system we want.

The rest of this book is devoted to explaining these principles:

1. Decide on the results we want.
   - use high standards.
   - set specific, measurable goals.
2. Adopt a plan to achieve those goals.
3. Give the local campus (i.e., principals and teachers) the authority to achieve those goals.
4. Measure academic results.
5. Reward results and insist upon consequences for failure.
6. Change what takes place in the classroom
   - encourage flexibility and experimentation
   - ensure a disciplined, drug-free environment
   - remember that virtues matter
7. Overhaul the school finance system. Refuse to put new money into the same old system until we create a new contract with taxpayers and a system that will reward their investment in education.
8. Get involved and stay involved in the schools.

These principles, remember, are interlocking and build on one another. Together, they will give us schools that are accountable, efficient, and excellent. Now let's see how a new school system would work.

CHAPTER 4

DECIDE ON THE RESULTS WE WANT

SET SPECIFIC, MEASURABLE GOALS

In January 1942, during the darkest moments of World War II, President Franklin D. Roosevelt delivered his State of the Union address. The nation was still reeling from the Japanese attack on Pearl Harbor, which dealt a devastating blow to our Pacific fleet.

It was a "now or never" moment. Because Americans needed bravery and determination, Roosevelt's speech rang with patriotic rhetoric.

But America needed something else as well. Isolationist policies after World War I had left us unprepared for war against powerful enemies. So Roosevelt did more than denounce our enemies and call for courage. He set specific, measurable goals for the nation in response to the crisis.

"We must raise our sights all along the production line," FDR said. "Let no man say it cannot be done."

"It" was a staggering set of production goals for 1942: sixty thousand planes, forty-five thousand tanks, twenty thousand antiaircraft guns, six million tons of merchant shipping. According to Doris Kearns Goodwin in her book *No Ordinary Time*, "The figures reached such astronomical proportions that human minds could not reach around them. Only by symbols could they be understood: a plane every four minutes…; a tank every seven minutes; two seagoing ships a day."[1]

Those were not low standards! As we all know, the goals were achieved. The "arsenal of democracy" soon began to turn the tide against the Axis powers.

Twenty years later, President Kennedy propelled America to the moon when he set a specific, measurable goal for the country:

"First, I believe that this nation should commit itself to achieving the goal, before the decade is out, of landing a man on the moon and returning him safely to the earth."[2]

Kennedy didn't say, "Let's put another man in orbit." He demanded more. As Roosevelt's wartime challenge had done, the sheer enormity of the goal inspired the nation. Note too that presidents Roosevelt and Kennedy did more than say, "Let us do our best" or "Let us succeed." They *defined what success would be* in terms that anyone could understand. Anything short of that would be failure.

The first step in transforming our school system is to establish specific, measurable goals. That means we must spell out in plain language what students should know and be able to do at different ages or grade levels. That is vital for at least four reasons:

1. We can't design the school system we want if we don't know the results we want. We must see the end in the beginning.

2. Without agreement on the critical element of the "product" we want, we can't know whether we are getting the job done.

3. If we don't agree on what we want to produce, we can't hold people accountable for success or failure.

4. If we don't decide what we want our students to know and be able to do, we can't begin to decide how much money we need to spend on public education. We have no intelligent basis on which to debate budget issues.

Imagine that you were starting a manufacturing business but had not decided what product to make—shoes, cars, video games, soap. How would you know what production system to put in place? How would you establish quality control procedures? Until you answered the key question—what are we making here?—you would be helpless.

That is roughly the situation our schools are in today. Because we have never decided on the goals we should strive to reach (the ends) we focus on controlling the *process* of education (the means). We stipulate which courses students must take to graduate—instead of spelling out what they should learn in those courses. The state buys textbooks and says schools may use only these textbooks—but what are students supposed to get from those textbooks?

Here is an example of a specific, measurable goal: *By the end of the third grade, every child will be reading at or above grade level.*

This is the type of goal we need. Virtually every educator will tell you that if a child does not learn to read by the third grade, the odds are overwhelming that the child will not succeed academically and will drop out of school. In short, if you do not teach the child to read by the third grade, you cannot spend enough on remedial education to catch up.

Such a clear, unambiguous goal—"by the end of the third grade, every child will be reading at or above grade level"—acts as a beacon light, or like the polestar that sailors navigate by. We know where it is and we know where we are. The presence of the goal forces us to determine not simply how to comply with state regulations, but how to change what we are doing if we're drifting off course.

There is the goal: Teach those kids to read by the end of the third grade. How? By any means necessary. If we must require that first graders who are lagging behind attend after-school tutoring sessions, so be it. If students need to spend more days in school, fine. Do they need tutors from the community? Okay, let's find the tutors.

Our school system now is like a family that sets off on vacation without any clear idea of where they want to go. They don't know whether they'll end up in Galveston, Hot Springs, or Tulsa, but they're arguing loudly about who gets to drive and whether to turn right or left.

This lack of clarity about goals allows our schools to commit consumer fraud.

• We still have "high school math" courses that are really futile attempts to teach students the math they should have learned in grade school.

• We have "honors" courses that years ago were standard courses for everyone.

• We ask too little of our best students. Several years ago a parent of a student in one of our state's most "successful" suburban school districts told me that his son, who was taking "honors" courses in every subject and maintaining an A average, was not required to read a single book from cover to cover during his entire ninth grade year!

• We have massive grade inflation. More than eighty percent of the 1.1 million U.S. students who took College Board exams in 1990 had a B or better grade point average. Yet forty percent of those students scored less than 390 on the verbal part of the SAT, thus indicating that they would fare poorly in college. And as college standards decline, grade inflation continues. The median grade for college undergraduates last year was an A minus. At Smith College 89.3 percent of students make As or Bs; that number is 82 percent at the University of Washington and 74 percent at Texas A&M.

Without any clear set of goals, you can name a course whatever you want. Without high standards, grades become meaningless symbols. And these failures make a mockery of education not just in high school but in college, where more students are taking "fluff" courses.

College Without Sweat
You can earn a B.A. without ever reading *Paradise Lost* or solving an equation. Here is the percentage of four-year institutions that do not require taking courses in–

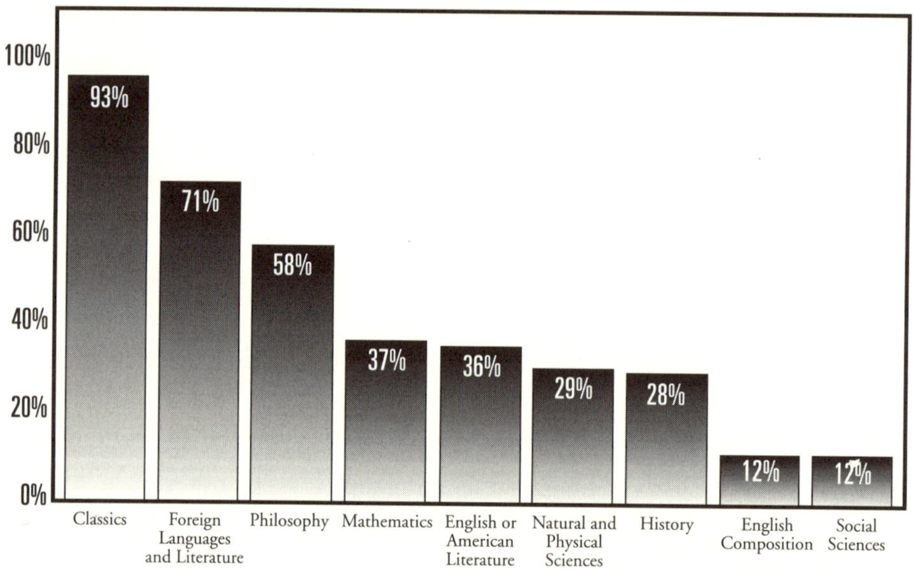

Source: U.S. News and World Report. May 28, 1990

Never have so many been so well rewarded for knowing so little. Until we spell out what our students should know and when, we have no way to judge the results.

The critical debate over goals and standards should not be left to educators alone. Taxpayers, parents, and the business community—small business as well as large—should have places at the table in order to give realistic input on the job skills high school graduates should possess.

Think of it as a three-tiered process. The first and critical step is to set high standards at the national level. This process began in Charlottesville, Virginia, in 1989 at the Governors' Education Summit, which agreed upon the national goals that were codified into law by Congress in 1994. Among the goals are the following. By the year 2000,

• all children in America will start school ready to learn.

• the high school graduation rate will increase to at least 90 percent from its current 71.2 percent.

• all students will leave grades 4, 8, and 12 having demonstrated competency over challenging subject matter including English, mathematics, science, foreign languages, civics, and so forth.

• United States students will be first in the world in mathematics and science achievement.[3]

(See Appendix, page 144 for a full list of the national goals.)

These national goals are necessarily broad but still useful as a general guide. Next, at the state and district levels, we must establish specific, measurable goals—the "what" we want our children to learn—and put in place a system to measure results and reward results. Then we leave the "how" to each school principal, because instructional decisions—the "how" versus the "what"—are most effectively made at the local level where the diverse needs of kids must be met.

ADOPT A PLAN

After we have decided on our goals, we should insist that those responsible at every level for our schools give us a plan for reaching them. The principal is responsible for the school plan, the superintendent for the district plan, and the Commissioner of Education for the state plan.

In making plans we need to be realistic. We will not achieve our goals overnight. But we must have a plan to get there. The plan should show, year by year, how we will reach our goals. Then each oversight body must monitor our progress against the plan, issuing interim reports on the results we're achieving.

Each person must be evaluated according to one overriding criterion: *How is he or she helping us to carry out the plan?* The school district superintendent, for example, must evaluate the campus principal according to the plan, not according to secondary criteria such as number of college degrees or years of experience or whether the principal is part of the old-boy network. If we focus solely on meeting our goals, we will promote an attitude of "whatever it takes" to succeed.

The presence of a plan also allows us to have an intelligent conversation about budgets. Today the budget process, at every level, consists of keeping every program in place until doomsday and arguing about how much more money can be squeezed out of the taxpayers. A sane system would tie expenses to the achievement of goals. For example, if one of our goals is to have all children computer literate by, say, the sixth grade, that obviously dictates certain expenses on computers at the elementary level.

Set High Standards and Get Results

For years when the subject of declining standards was raised, educators balked, arguing that imposing high academic standards on all high school students would create greater educational inequality and accentuate educational disparities between socioeconomic and racial groups.

But newer thinking seems to show just the opposite: High standards bring high performance. A recent article published in *The American Educator* demolishes the arguments for lowering the bar, citing a comprehensive study conducted for the U.S. Department of Education:

> It is clear that equal educational opportunity was not achieved by lowering academic standards through curricular differentiation, tracking, shortening courses from two semesters to one, and giving academic credit to previously extracurricular activities. Indeed, the students most harmed by these policies were the children of working class and minority families.[4]

Even the most disadvantaged students will respond positively if someone holds them to high standards. At Hostos-Lincoln Academy of Science in the South Bronx, one of the nation's poorest neighborhoods, a special program was established seven years ago for at-risk students, many of whom had been labeled dropout material by their middle-school counselors. The academy offers small classes and lots of individual attention, but the key is a demanding program of college-level work. "At first we felt students couldn't do it, but we were wrong," the school's principal told *Newsweek*. In fact, the students nearly doubled their reading scores over two years. They take trigonometry, not consumer math, and the number of students in each class who passed the state's regents' biology test rose from nine to fifty percent in two years. Best of all, about seventy percent of the class of 1989 graduated on time, double the city's average. About eighty percent plan to attend college.[5]

At Georgia Tech, it was much the same story. For years

the college had been offering a largely remedial orientation program with little success in improving the performance of blacks and Hispanics. In 1989 the college adopted a rigorous summer course for minority freshmen, that included calculus and chemistry.

"The change was in us and what we told them we expected of them," the president of the college told the *New York Times.* "In the past we told them they were dumb, that they needed fixing, and we had them in remedial programs." Under the new program, spurred on by higher standards, students in the program have raised their grade point averages as high as 3.0—slightly higher than the school average—and have virtually erased the "performance gap" between minority engineering students and their white counterparts.[6]

The Reverend Jesse Jackson and I do not see eye to eye on every subject, but we totally agree that teachers must have high expectations for their students. On the first day of sixth grade, Jackson once told a reporter, his teacher began writing long, unfamiliar words on the blackboard.

Somebody finally called out, "Uh, Miz Shelton? Those are the eighth grade words. We only the sixth grade here."

The teacher didn't miss a beat.

"I know what grade I am teaching," she told the class. "And you'll learn every one of these words and a lot more like 'em, before this year is over. I will not teach down to you. One of you little brats just might be mayor or governor or even President some day and I'm gonna make sure you'll be ready."[7]

LOW STANDARDS, LOW SKILLS, LOW WAGES

As a wise person once said, "You will never exceed your own expectations." Jesse Jackson's teacher was not afraid to set high standards, and we must do the same. When we do, we should take a long look at alarming figures like this.

In Texas today, we have more than 150,000 students enrolled in home economics and almost 80,000 students enrolled in agriculture vocational education![8] That might make sense for the economy of 1955, but not the economy we have in 1995. As we move into an Information Society that demands increasingly sophisticated thinking skills, it's amazing that we have so many students spending time in such courses. They say that generals often fight the previous war. These students are preparing for the job market of the previous century.

The average Texas worker will probably be employed by at least five different companies and hold ten or more different positions before retiring. It is estimated that three-quarters of the new jobs created in Texas in the next decade will require solid reading, writing, and math skills as well as creative thinking, responsibility, and innovation. That means even harder times for the 53,420 students who left Texas schools without graduating in the 1992–93 school year. The typical high school dropout, who might have had a fair chance of landing a decent job a decade ago, will not have much of a chance in the decade ahead.

Because we have not been specific enough about what results we want from our schools, for too long our answer has been to lower the bar when anyone has difficulties. So we "dumb down" our curriculum and use social promotion to pass unprepared students to the next grade. As a result, we have high school graduates who cannot meet today's rising standards. Sadly, they will find that in business there is no social promotion.

One promising program making some headway in raising

standards in Texas schools is the Texas Scholars project, sponsored by the Texas Business and Education Coalition. The Texas Scholars program encourages schools to offer students a more rigorous set of graduation requirements than the minimum requirements set by state law. Texas Scholars, for instance, must take more demanding math courses, including algebra I and II and geometry; and science courses such as biology, chemistry, and physics.

The Texas Scholars program begins in the eighth grade, educating parents and students to the reality that in today's world, minimum standards do not result in good jobs for good wages after graduation. Because of the student demand generated by the Scholars programs, the State Board of Education was forced to incorporate the essence of the program into a "recommended high school" program. Sooner rather than later, everyone should be expected to reach this higher standard.

Don't be Afraid of Outcomes!

Only by defining the academic results we want can we have accountability in education. We must emphasize results, not how much we spent per child or the average salaries for teachers. And we cannot allow this proper emphasis on academic results to become embroiled in the growing controversy over "outcome-based education" or OBE.

The flap over OBE sprang up when education policy makers as diverse as William Bennett and Albert Shanker began to push for an emphasis on the outcome of a student's education—the academic results. The educational bureaucrats' answer was to emasculate the concept and mire the whole discussion in a confusing argument.

What we need, of course, are specific, measurable goals. Instead, they established nebulous, intangible outcomes like these examples from Pennsylvania, where the desired results were defined in part as follows:

Goal: Self-Worth

All students understand and appreciate their worth as unique and capable individuals and exhibit self-esteem. All students act through a desire to succeed rather than a fear of failure while recognizing that failure is part of everyone's experiences.[9]

It's easy to see what's wrong with such a "goal." How in the world would a teacher measure progress toward this goal, or decide when a student was acting "through a desire to succeed rather than a fear of failure…"? Do you think students might be tempted to say they had the right "desire" in order to pass the course?

Goal: Arts and Humanities

All students advocate the preservation and promotion of cultural heritage and traditions, including works of art, presentations and performances in the local and global community as a function of good citizenship.[10]

Does "advocate" here mean students will publicly proclaim the need to preserve and promote, and so forth? Or does it simply mean they will favor it? Are all "traditions" worth preserving?

In Minnesota one exit outcome defined a successful graduate as "a community contributor who appreciates and understands diversity." It is not immediately clear what this outcome means, how it would be taught, or how it would be measured.

In short, the concept of outcome-based education has been hijacked and twisted into something it was never meant to be. Even worse, it has been turned into a political football. Groups such as Phyllis Schlafly's Eagle Forum and Pat Robertson's Christian Coalition strongly oppose outcome based education, fearing that amorphous "outcomes" will lead to public schools promoting values that are anathema to families. When well-meaning families are confused by this rhetoric, that gives school boards an excuse to drop the whole subject. (To placate such critics, the incoming superintendent of one Dallas-area school district recently announced that he would *not* follow the OBE philosophy he had embraced in another district.) The right answer, of course, is to make the "outcomes" academically related, not to give in to the forces that have hijacked and distorted the objective.

I can anticipate some questions about results: "Okay, you say we have to spell out the results we want from our schools. We have to define the education we want our children to have. So what should it be? How much English, how much math, how much computer science, how much PE, and so forth? Where's the Tom Luce Curriculum for Tomorrow?"

That's a fair question. Like everyone who is concerned with our schools, I have my opinions and preferences about the skills and knowledge our graduates should possess. But I've not stressed those ideas in this book because I believe the real "Curriculum for Tomorrow" should emerge from a statewide consensus-building program. That consensus should feature healthy debate and be shaped by parents, educators, the business community, elected leaders, and others.

Remember: Winning the battle for specific, measurable goals and high standards is absolutely crucial if we are to radically restructure our schools. That's because accountability is the missing ingredient in education today. The buck stops nowhere. And you cannot have accountability if you do not have goals and standards.

Even more important, goals and standards will free teachers and principals to be the professionals they want to be. Each teacher will determine *how* students can best learn once we have decided *what* they must learn. And that's the next step: giving real authority to those who will be responsible for bringing about the results we want.

Give Authority to Those Responsible for Results

❖

"Help the Principals Win for the Kids"

Let me share with you a letter I recently received from a principal in the Houston Independent School District. For reasons that will be clear, the principal must remain anonymous.

In my experience, site-based management and shared decision-making means, "We in the central office are going to make this decision and 'share' it with you. You will have to manage the results at your site."

I wish principals really could get the right teachers and run off the bad ones. While it may be part of Senate Bill 1 that no teacher be assigned to a school without the principal's approval, in actual practice this is not the case. Time after time, poor teachers are merely shifted from one campus to another.

How can I be held accountable for the learning of students in a class taught by a teacher with a history of ineffectiveness, who was assigned to my school by the Personnel Department against my wishes? In this particular case (and most school districts are full of such instances), this teacher missed forty-one days in the first semester. In any for-profit business such absenteeism would never be tolerated, nor would gross ineffectiveness.

I believe with all my heart that my school would be extremely effective, without pouring additional money into it, if I did have the power to hire and fire.

The good teachers in my school are extremely good, and I do my best to protect them, praise them and provide them with what they need. In return they are cooperative, supportive and dedicated.

The poor teachers do the bare minimum and remain in the school district because it has become far too difficult to fire them. Principals become burned out from expending time and energy, futilely trying to get these ineffective teachers removed from their schools—time and energy that could be better spent interacting in positive ways.

Help the principals win for the kids. I know we can make a difference.

This glimpse of a principal's life reinforces what I learned back in 1984 when I studied what was working in successful schools. It also underscores the fact that we haven't solved the problems that vex our principals. Site-based management—granting principals more autonomy—has become the law, but in reality, little progress has been made in decentralizing authority and decision-making. The central administration continues to cling to power; the campus principal doesn't have the budget authority she needs or the power to hire and fire personnel, free from central office control and without years of legal wrangling. So far, true site-based management is about as scarce as portraits of Jimmy Johnson in Jerry Jones's office.

STRONG PRINCIPALS MEAN STRONG SCHOOLS

My search for successful schools began when the Select Committee asked me to find the schools that were getting the job done across the country and study what they were doing.

That approach made sense to me—find the good schools, then isolate the characteristics that make them successful. So I began to study schools in Texas and the rest of the country, building a list of high-performing campuses. What I found surprised me at first.

The conventional wisdom has long held that such factors as amount of money spent, ethnic makeup, and family income determined a school's success. But we were finding role-model schools all over the economic and social spectrum, in every kind of environment, with every kind of student population. In the roughest, most impoverished ghetto or the most remote rural area, certain schools were achieving. Often these schools were spending the same as or less than their peers.

Why? It was quickly apparent that these good schools did not owe their success to a particular ethnic makeup, amount of money spent, or family income. In other words, most of the factors that we have long believed determine academic results are not as important as we may have thought.

But all those successful schools, whatever their economic status or location, shared one vitally important characteristic. The common denominator of successful schools, we found, was a principal who was an academic leader—and who had found a way around "the system." That should tell us something about the system, when its most capable principals can only succeed by circumventing the frustrating, time-wasting regulations that choke innovation and experimentation.

Likewise, academic research confirms the importance of the principal. "More than any other figure, the principal is able to create conditions for excellence," says Professor James Guthrie of the University of California–Berkeley. "If you could only change one component of a school in order to make it more effective, finding a dynamic principal is the most important thing you can do."

Unfortunately, the successful principal in today's schools must be a rebel, a guerrilla fighter who has finally decided that his or her students are worth battling the status quo. It's our job to change the system so that principals don't have to spend their valuable time and energy mopping up after incompetent teachers or jumping bureaucratic hurdles. Instead, let's help them turn that energy to improving classroom learning.

IT'S THE PRINCIPAL, STUPID

One of the memorable quotes from the 1992 presidential campaign was "It's the economy, stupid." Bill Clinton's political advisors used that line as a sort of mantra to keep themselves focused, in the chaos of the campaign, on what they saw as the voters' primary concern and the winning issue.

It worked for the Clinton campaign, and it gave me an idea. In the past two years I've given out scores of coffee cups with "It's the Principal, Stupid" lettered on them. After all, the principal's job is where the rubber meets the road.

How important is the principal? All-important. If the principal is doing her job,

- the school will be focused on learning,
- good teachers will be recruited,
- teachers will be allowed to do their jobs as professionals,

- discipline will be enforced,
- bad teachers will be reassigned,
- parents will be involved in the school, and
- students will take part in an exciting learning process.

Alas. As we all know, those conditions don't exist in most schools today. On most of our campuses, the principal cannot hire or fire staffers. She cannot determine how money is spent or which textbooks are used. In fact, principals are hamstrung when it comes to almost all of the decisions a real leader needs to make. They have the headaches, but not the authority to solve problems. It's one hell of a way to run a railroad. We've got to change that and make site-based management a reality.

When we change our school system, we must recognize the vital importance of the principal—the CEO of the school—in a number of ways. First, we should make the principal the highest paid administrator in the school district after the superintendent. No coordinator of curriculum, deputy assistant for middle-school procurement, or football coach should earn more than the CEO of a school.

Second, we must do away with the current process by which men and women train to become principals. Today it's really a matter of self-selection. Teacher Bob Smith knows that he can make more money as a principal than as a teacher, so he scoots off to the local university, gets an administration degree, and hires on as principal of Bigtown High. Bob may lack both the skills and the temperament for the job, but here he is. The people charged with his training have little to do with the real-world schools in which he will operate. In business, by contrast, promising candidates for upper management are groomed by senior executives who can evaluate their talents and insist that they improve in areas where they are deficient.

Third, principals need better development and training for their roles both before and after they get their administration degrees. They need a broader set of skills than principals have traditionally brought to their schools. They need to know how to train personnel, how to motivate people, how to build teams, how to budget and make their way through a balance sheet. Local businesses could play a role here by taking principals into their management training programs during the summers.

LET'S END THE TOP-DOWN TYRANNY

I learned something else very revealing about our schools back in 1984 while working on the recommendations that became House Bill 72. We wanted to be sure we had input from the soldiers on the front lines—the teachers. So we hired a nationally recognized consulting firm to conduct the largest survey ever of the opinions and attitudes of Texas teachers.

The firm had previously done employee surveys in organizations all over the country, ranging from IBM to the assembly line at General Motors to garbage collectors in New York City. But the Texas results shocked the consultants. They reported that the morale of Texas teachers was the worst they had ever measured in any organization—including those garbage workers in New York City![1] Keep in mind this was in 1984, before juvenile crime and violence had multiplied in our cities and schools.

The reason for this widespread unhappiness? Heading the list was the organizational structure of the schools. Texas schools were the most top-down, autocratic organizations imaginable. Authority flowed only one way—from the Legislature and the TEA, to school boards and central administrations, down to the schools. Mandates and edicts came down from on high; input from principals and teachers, the troops on the front lines, was almost never sought, seldom received, and almost never acted upon.

Naturally, teachers felt stifled. They were treated as automatons or trained animals—hired hands, not hired minds. They were not seen as real professionals but as flunkies carrying out orders. In school hallways from Brownsville to Sherman, you would hear teachers talking about a problem created by "Austin." The teachers sounded hopeless and helpless. Theirs not to reason why; theirs but to carry out the will of "Austin."

In addition to the top-down tyranny, teachers were frustrated by the proliferation of paperwork and by the lack of time for planning, staff development, and growth. They complained about having too little time for interaction with teachers from other grades or feeder schools. Indeed, too often our schools treat each grade level as absolutely distinct from every other level, as if a fourth grader is going to spend the rest of his life, not just 180 days, in the fourth grade. Teachers have no time to work with other grade teachers to develop a seamless system for the kids.

AUTHORITY MEANS ACCOUNTABILITY

For too long, weak principals and teachers have rationalized their ineffectiveness by saying they don't really have the power to change things. "I just work here, Mac," their attitude seems to say. The buck stops nowhere—and everywhere. There is no real accountability.

Under the system we must build, there will be accountability all the way down the line. We must give the principal the power to act as CEO of the school—but with power comes responsibility and accountability: Within a certain time span, she must produce or face the consequences of failure. And one cautionary note: Principals cannot get caught up in new struggles over a new control mechanism—the "school councils" that are now being formed. Principals have a responsibility to consult with parents and teachers, but that does not mean diffusing authority and responsibility that should lie with the CEO of the school. The buck must stop somewhere; I say it should stop at the principal's desk.

Because the schools are still modeled on the paradigm of the nineteenth-century factory, where omnipotent bosses handed down orders to assembly-line drones, giving authority to those responsible for results—teachers and principals—will require a radical shift in our thinking.

Our hierarchical, bureaucratic mind set fosters a "one size fits all" approach to education that permeates everything our schools do. As a result, we've lost sight of the fact that one size does not fit all! Texas school children come in every size and shape and color, with educational needs that defy a cookie-cutter approach.

The educational strategies of a rural school district, an inner city school, and a suburban school may need to vary greatly–but they cannot if we do not decentralize our system. Principals must be freed from the nightmare of urban central administrations so they can create distinctive instructional programs for their distinctive children.

In turn, that principal will insist that each classroom teacher be allowed to perform as a professional, using his or her expertise and discretion to tailor instruction that suits individual students. If a teacher thinks that one of his ninth-grade history classes needs to spend three class periods on Lincoln's Gettysburg Address, while another class needs only two class periods, that should be the teacher's decision.

This philosophy recognizes the teacher as a professional. Lawyers do not treat every client the same way. Doctors fine-tune their treatment according to the patient's individual needs and history. By the same token, teachers must be free to bring their professional skills to bear on different students in different ways.

Decentralization is vital to real reform of the schools. But a word of caution. *Decentralizing the current system without these other reforms could be disastrous.* Decentralization will do us little good unless we set high standards and specific goals, assess results, reward results, and insist on accountability. If we yield to the siren song of decentralization without first establishing goals and accountability, there is nothing to prevent the liberated schools from dumbing down their curricula or pouring inordinate sums of money into football.

Decentralization may come in stages, but we'll know it's really arrived when state funding goes directly to a campus (see Chapter 8) to be spent as the principal sees fit. The rhetoric of independence must be backed up with real autonomy not just in matters of instruction, hiring, and firing, but in budgetary matters. Local campuses should be free to buy resources from the central office, from a college of education, from IBM, or any other supplier. Central administrative offices would become leaner and more effective if their continued existence was dependent upon the "customer"—the local campus.

Schools That Work

Whenever I feel discouraged about the fight to build great schools, I think of three great principals who are winning the fight for their kids.

• St. Philip's is located in one of the most impoverished neighborhoods in Dallas. The principal or headmaster of the school is Terry Flowers, who grew up in a similar neighborhood in Chicago. For years the school had to contend with a crack house next door because city officials dragged their feet on enforcing city codes.

Despite all the obstacles, St. Philip's provides a quality education for about two hundred students from pre-kindergarten through the fourth grade. Eighty-five percent of St. Philip's students perform at or higher than grade level. St. Philip's does all this for a cost of about $1,000 less per pupil than the Dallas Independent School District's average cost of $4,432. Pay and benefits for the staff are less than in the DISD, yet the staff experiences little turnover because teachers feel good about what they are doing. They are allowed to be the professionals they want to be.

St. Philip's is a busy place around the clock, also serving as a community center and coordinating housing programs for senior citizens, family literacy programs, Meals on Wheels, a health clinic, parenting classes, and summer programs for kids.

"St. Philip's students achieve because they are expected to achieve," says Terry Flowers. "It's not fair to compare us against public schools because we have the freedom to make certain demands on students and parents that public schools can't. *They could, but politically, they won't.*" (Italics added)

• East Dallas Community School (EDCS) was formed some sixteen years ago by a young lady named Terry Ford. Terry, a graduate of SMU, had always wanted to be a school teacher, but she lasted only five years in Dallas public schools before she burned out from fighting—and losing—the battles for what her kids needed.

But she did not abandon her dream of teaching. She formed a school of her own in 1978 for the purpose of showing that all children, regardless of race or income level, can succeed in school when given a challenging and supportive educational program.

The enrollment at EDCS is balanced between African-Americans, Hispanics and Anglo. Seventy-five percent of the children are from low-income families. Still, a recent study reported that EDCS students scored in the top twenty-five per-cent of students nationwide on standardized tests. An amazing ninety-six percent of those who attend EDCS for three or more years maintain at least a B average and thirty-five percent maintain an A average. The school spends $3,921 per pupil, less than Dallas Independent School District schools. More than 450 students are on a waiting list to get in.

• For several years I have had the pleasure of attending a series of remarkable sessions with successful principals from across Texas. Under the auspices of the Principals' Network, these men and women get together to share ideas on making their schools work. One of the most fascinating members of the group is Thaddeus S. Lott, principal of Mabel B. Wesley Elementary School in Northwest Houston.

The students at Wesley are ninety-nine percent minority and almost ninety percent of them come from families whose income is below poverty guidelines, qualifying the youngsters for the free lunch program. But nobody at Mabel Wesley grabs for the convenient excuse that minority kids from low-income families can't succeed. Thaddeus's children consistently produce reading and math test scores in the top eightieth to ninetieth percentile of all schools in the Houston Independent School District—rich or poor. Wesley students average one grade level above the grade they are in.

What is the secret of Thaddeus Lott's success? It's simple. His educational philosophy is "Students, given the opportunity, can learn—and that means all students." And he knows that opportunity can't exist without order. His school is a model of discipline, where the children enter each day walking in lines.

When Thaddeus took over at Wesley, the first thing he did was tell the existing teacher corps that he expected an extraordinary degree of commitment and hard work. Teachers were expected to plan well and teach well. Thaddeus did not hesitate to tell teachers who could not measure up to go elsewhere. In one of our sessions with principals from across the state, one new principal from Dallas was so inspired by the example of Thaddeus's school that she replaced ten non-performing teachers over the next month. Because of her actions, one year later her school was removed from the state's "low-performing" category.

It can be done if the leader expects it to be done. These principals do. There is no doubt in my mind that these men and women are making a difference, but we've got to help them by setting goals and building a plan for reaching those goals.

Remember: "It's the principal, stupid." Once authority has been given to those who are really responsible for achieving the goals, we're ready for the next step: measuring and rewarding results.

CHAPTER 6

MEASURE AND REWARD RESULTS

REPORT CARDS: A FIRST STEP

Each year, publicly owned corporations compile a report on virtually every aspect of their business and release the report to shareholders. It's the law, and it makes perfect sense. Shareholders have rights. They need information to help them decide whether to continue or enlarge their investment in the company. Without that information, they're flying blind.

Unfortunately, the shareholders in our public schools have been flying blind for years. I'm talking, of course, about the parents and other taxpayers who support the schools with their hard-earned money. For much too long, that money went into the schools via Austin and local property taxes, but very little information came *out* of the schools to help the "shareholders" evaluate their investment.

When we were struggling over House Bill 72 back in 1983–84, parents had nothing beyond word of mouth to rely on if they wanted to evaluate a school or compare one school to another. Now there has been some progress.

For the first time, in the fall of 1994, every school campus was required to send to its parents a school report card containing valuable information about the school. Among other things, the report card shows TAAS results by subject, grade, and student group, and also shows how each school ranks in a selected group of one hundred similar schools, and in the state as a whole. The card also gives other information such as percentages of students taking the SAT and ACT tests and how they scored, dropout rates, attendance rates, program enrollment (how many enroll in special education programs, how many in gifted and talented programs, and so forth). There is also information about how much money the school receives and, generally, how it is spent. (See Appendix, pages 145–153 for a sample card and detailed explanation.)

This report card represents an important first step toward full disclosure—but it's only a first step. Those who fought the battle for this report card deserve loud applause, but we can't stop there.

To have truly meaningful assessment, we must first put our specific, measurable goals in place and lay out a year-by-year plan to achieve those goals. Then the report card should reveal every school's progress toward meeting the goals. Until we have those goals, we can't really measure whether we're succeeding or failing.

That's because school is a place where learning *can* happen, just as a hospital is a place where healing can happen. But you can sit in a hospital all day long and not get well until you and the doctor decide on a goal, whether it's treating your asthma or bandaging your sprained wrist. Likewise, you can sit in school all day—and thus be counted as a live, breathing body on attendance rolls—and never succeed if there are no specific goals.

Information Is Power: The Report Card We Need

Our current confusion about assessment reminds me of old Casey Stengel the year he took over the fledgling New York Mets, who would set a record for most losses by a major league team. "I managed good," quipped the Ole Perfessor, "but they sure played bad."

Unfortunately, it doesn't work that way in baseball or education. If a manager's players "play bad," then by definition he is not "managing good," because the goal is to win games. If a teacher's students aren't learning, then the teacher is not teaching well, no matter how many degrees he has, how long he has taught, or how much money we are spending on schools.

I can hear the question: "But how can you spot the really effective teachers as opposed to those who are not performing? How can you know who is really succeeding and who is just filling a space?"

It's no longer a matter of guesswork. Not many people know it, but today in many districts the data exists—and should exist in all districts—to measure precisely how much learning is taking place and find the obstacles to improvement. That data, if properly publicized, will give parents vital knowledge—and that in itself will force change.

The best system I know of for evaluating that data was jointly designed by the Dallas Independent School District, the Dallas Citizens Council, and the Greater Dallas Chamber of Commerce. Their effort has produced a useful, concise management reporting system that will quantify for the principal of any school how well the school is doing. Even more important, it will show the principal precisely where efforts to improve performance must be focused.

A complete sample School Performance Management

report is included in the Appendix on pages 154–164. Please take a few minutes to read it. When you do, you will immediately see that second grade reading is the weak link in this school, ranking at the twentieth percentile.

But the analysis does not stop there. The page for Level 3 shows us the second grade classes in our sample school averaged only six months of academic gain for nine months of school. As we all know, however, averages can be terribly misleading. This report reveals that one teacher (class 2C) actually had thirteen months of academic gain in nine months of school. The second grade's average was pulled down by another teacher (class 2A) whose students had only two months of academic gain for nine months of classes!

This report has a clear message for the principal: If you really want to improve your academic results, the teacher of class 2A has to go—and the teacher of class 2C deserves a large pay raise. Remember, these are teachers in the same school, serving the same types of kids. In fact, in this example the kids who entered the low-performing class 2A actually were operating at a higher level when they entered the second grade than the kids who entered the high-performing class 2C.

This report vividly illustrates the "value added" by a great teacher and the harmful impact of a poor teacher. Almost all the students unlucky enough to be assigned to class 2C ended the year further behind than when they entered the second grade.

This is the kind of exacting information that a real report card should give parents and taxpayers: How many students are functioning at grade level, above grade level, and below grade level? Which teachers are moving the enterprise forward, and which ones are not? And how are our students performing on nationally normed tests? If people buying cars are told how many miles per gallon they will get, and people buying frozen tacos know how many grams of fat are in each taco, why shouldn't parents of school children be told about a teacher's strengths and weaknesses?

There are other flaws in the TEA report card. For years the education establishment fought a rear-guard action against meaningful assessment. First there was no assessment available to the public. Then, when their backs were against the wall, they gave us a Texas-only test.

Well, Texas is big, but our kids live in a world much larger than Texas. The measurement tool we need will also tell us how they are doing against students in other states and against students in foreign countries. Our students will compete for jobs against graduates from California, Florida, Arizona, England, and Japan. We need to know how they stack up.

Then there is the "similar schools" problem. The current campus report card perpetuates the worst kind of discrimination by comparing poor schools against poor schools, rural schools against rural schools, and so on.

Earth to bureaucrats: Our students will not spend the rest of their lives in ghettoized categories like "poor" and "rural." They will compete for jobs with youngsters from all over the state, the country, and the world. There will be no jobs set aside for the rural poor, and if they fall short on the job these graduates will not be able to say, "I'm from a poor little school, so give me a break."

We must expect more from every school, regardless of average family income and geographical region. We must not tolerate different standards for different parts of the state!

THE WHOLE STORY: MONEY, CLASS SIZE, CREDENTIALS

A transformed school system will need a report card that not only shows progress toward academic goals, but reveals specifically how each campus spends taxpayer money. The current TEA report card lists expenditures per student on instruction (mostly teacher salaries), administration (mostly principals' salaries), and so forth. That allows taxpayers to know that School X spent, say, \$1,919 per student on instruction while the school district average was \$2,702 and the state average was \$2,549.

Unfortunately, that information is of limited value unless we know how much we are spending per academic course, how much we spend per vocation education course, and how much we are spending for each extracurricular activity. We will never establish priorities for our money until we have real cost accounting per activity.

A painfully vivid example of our misplaced priorities comes from G. H. Bissenger's 1990 book *Friday Night Lights*, a penetrating study of the ways that high school football dominates the Ector School District. According to Bissenger, the Mojo-mad Odessa-Permian High School spends more to get football game film developed a day early than it spends on instructional materials for all of its English courses.[1] And Odessa-Permian is not alone. State Comptroller John Sharp, in his recent report titled *Forces of Change*, tells of one school lamenting its inability to afford a physics teacher. Meanwhile, the school employed eighteen football coaches.[2]

Beyond dollars and cents, we need meaningful information about all kinds of things that happen in our schools. How many students were arrested? How many weapons were confiscated? And what about class sizes? What are the real class sizes—not an average size, but how many classrooms in what subjects or grades had how many students?

It's one thing to report "average" class sizes, but averages don't always tell the most important truths. Labor Secretary Robert Reich, who stands four feet ten inches, often makes that point by noting that he and basketball player Shaquille O'Neal (seven feet two inches) have an average height of six feet. Of course, everyone knows you can drown in a lake with an average depth of three feet.

How many parents know, for instance, that our state's vocational education classes have a student-teacher ratio that is substantially lower than the ratio in regular academic classes? That tells us that a vocational education student is much more likely to get extra attention from a teacher than is a student in sophomore English or math. Does that reflect the priorities we want in our schools?

We also need to know how many teachers are really certified for the courses they teach. I do not believe certification ought to be required and I know it doesn't guarantee a good teacher, but it seems strange for the education establishment to proclaim that certification is vital and then refuse to tell the public how many teachers are actually certified in the subjects they teach. Every report card ought to list all courses the athletic staff is teaching. We need to know if a school is hiding a football coach in the history classroom.

BETTER TESTS, NOT FEWER TESTS

As I've traveled around the state over the past few years, meeting scores of educators, I've heard endless complaints about the testing program. Over and over, teachers bemoan the fact that we have tests and cringe at the publicity the press gives the TAAS tests. They say they are forced to "teach to the test." The implication is that students are robbed of real learning because teachers must spend endless hours drumming rote information into their heads, which can then be regurgitated on The Test.

My response is this: First, real professionals will not let someone else tell them how to teach. Second, if teachers are indeed spending so much time teaching to the test, somebody tell me why students are doing so poorly on the test! Finally, the tests are designed to cover material in the curriculum. So of course the teachers are teaching to the test. And what is wrong with that? That simply means they are teaching their students the curriculum.

The problem is not that we have tests. The more valid criticism is that the tests are not tough enough or comprehensive enough. We ought to strive every year to strengthen and improve our testing, starting with our over-reliance on multiple-choice tests.

Our goal should be authentic assessment that will allow the teacher to determine whether a student has developed skills or acquired knowledge through the instruction program which can be applied in real-life situations. This might include solving real problems, actual use of equipment in a science lab, written essays, and so forth.

Eventually, we should test students at the beginning of the school year and again at the end of the school year. That will help us determine the "value added" by a school and a teacher. And it's the fair way to take into account the different starting points of various students.

Let's have a healthy debate over the value of different testing vehicles. Let's look for better tests, smarter tests, more inclusive tests—but let's accept the fact that tests are inevitable because taxpayers will not continue to increase the amount of money spent on education without assessment and accountability. Educators owe it to us to suggest a better system of testing instead of just moaning about the current system.

WE MUST STOP REWARDING FAILURE

Today our school finance system rewards failure, not results. For years the Legislature has fought about where we would get more money for so-called poor districts. But the additional funds, whether they came from "Robin Hood" or "Son of Robin Hood" or the Sheriff of Nottingham, were placed in the same old school finance distribution system that rewards failure instead of success. Let me give you three examples.

Failure Number 1: We give schools extra money to put kids in what we call "vocational education" rather than keep them on an academic track. Under the school finance distribution system now in use, schools receive 137 percent more for each student in vocational education[3]—a nice financial incentive for schools to convince kids to take vocational education courses.

Unfortunately, in too many instances schools train youngsters for jobs that do not exist or teach them skills that have become outmoded. School districts simply do not have the resources to invest in the capital-intensive equipment, nor the means to keep up to date and effectively train young people for the high-tech jobs of today. The "vocational education" that employers want young people to have today consists of first-rate reading, writing, and math skills. The employers will take care of the job-specific training in the workplace.

Failure Number 2: We give schools more money to keep young people in bilingual education than to graduate them from bilingual classes. That's why we have young people who never become proficient in English, the language of the workplace. This money rewards failure. A sane system would create financial incentives for schools that do a good job in making their students truly bilingual—speaking English and their native tongue—and moving them on to the regular program. That's a win-win situation.

Failure Number 3: We give schools more money to label children as special education projects. That is one reason why the number of students categorized as special education rose from 5.6 percent of the school population in 1969 to 12 percent of the school population in 1991. In the 1991–92 school year, 340,919 students were enrolled in special education classes. We need a system that does not give schools a financial incentive to label kids. Every child should receive a "special education."[4]

Speaking of misplaced priorities, if we pay for what we value, we're sending a very clear signal that we don't much value our gifted students. The proof? According to recent research, some seventy percent of federal spending on elementary and secondary education goes to the disadvantaged and handicapped. If you add in the spending for bilingual education and vocational programs, the share goes above eighty percent.

While myriad government programs benefit those deemed disadvantaged and handicapped, there is exactly *one* federal program that focuses on above-average students—and its share of elementary and secondary funding has never risen above one-tenth of one percent. In 1993, the Department of Education reported that state and local expenditures aimed at gifted and talented students hovered at around *two cents out of every one hundred dollars.*

Of course, we owe disadvantaged and handicapped students a good education—but it's a huge mistake to assume that the brighter students will somehow muddle through on their own without help or financial backing.

LET'S REWARD EXCELLENCE—INCENTIVES WORK!

We must change the school finance distribution system to pay schools not for failure but success. If a school's students show improvement in learning, let's give that school more money, not less. Conversely, if a school is not improving, why should we throw more money into the school? A system that really measures improvement gives everyone the chance to win.

For an incentive system that rewards results, consider Albert Shanker's idea for a contest every three years to determine which schools have made the biggest leaps in educational attainment. The winners (the top ten percent of the schools) would receive substantial bonuses for every employee who was part of the team effort. Shanker proposes $30,000 per employee—more than many teachers make in a year. Now that is an incentive system!

The program that best combines high standards and rewards for results is the Advanced Placement program in Ellis County, Texas, designed and funded by the O'Donnell Foundation of Dallas for the past five years. The program, which began as a way of luring top scientists and mathematicians to Ellis County to work on the Superconducting Super Collider, has improved student learning across the board in the participating schools. Similar programs should be implemented in schools across the state.

The goals of the program are clearly stated:
• Increase the number of high school graduates who are academically prepared to enter college and earn a degree.
• Motivate more young people to study science and math, especially in grades 7 through 12.
• Increase the number of students who pass the Advanced Placement exam in math, science, and English.

Financial incentives are provided to teachers, students, and schools for Advanced Placement courses in English, calculus, biology, chemistry, physics, and computer science.

ADVANCED PLACEMENT INCENTIVE PROGRAM

TEACHERS: • $1000 signing bonus when they teach their first AP course.

      • $250 stipend and all fees to attend AP Summer Institutes at colleges and universities.

      • $100 stipend and all fees to attend two-day AP teacher training conferences.

- AP calculus teachers receive TI-82 graphing calculators for their AP students, as well as a TI-82 View Screen.

STUDENTS:
- $100 scholarship for each AP exam score of 3 or 4.
- $200 scholarship for each AP exam score of 5.
- $30 toward the cost of each AP exam.
- The full exam fee, $71, is reimbursed for each score of 3 or over.
- Students scoring three or over on AP calculus receive a TI-85 graphing calculator.

SCHOOLS:
- $100 for each exam with a score of 3 or over to be used to strengthen and expand the AP program.

Notice that students are only rewarded for passing the test (a score of three, four, or five is passing on a scale of five). And the AP test gives us a way of comparing Texas students to students elsewhere. Because the AP test is a national test, a three in

SSC School Advanced Placement Exam Trends
Five Academic Years ended 1993-94

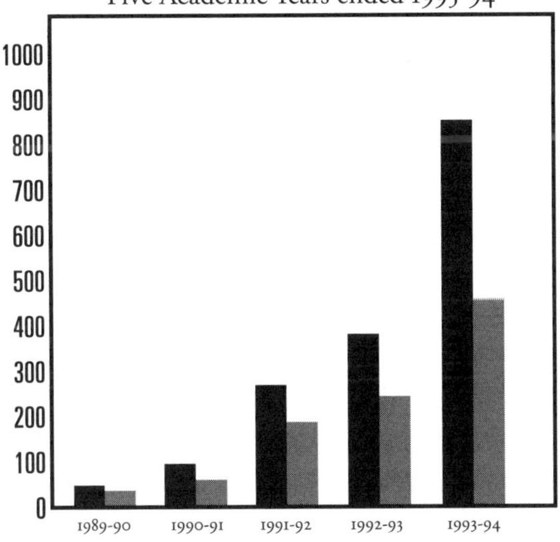

NOTE: For 1989-90 to 1992-93, test results are only for English, calculus, biology, chemistry, and physics. In 1993-94, computer science was added, and accounts for 73 exams. The AP Incentive Program began in 1990-91.

Source: The College Board

# of AP Exams   # Scores of 3 and up

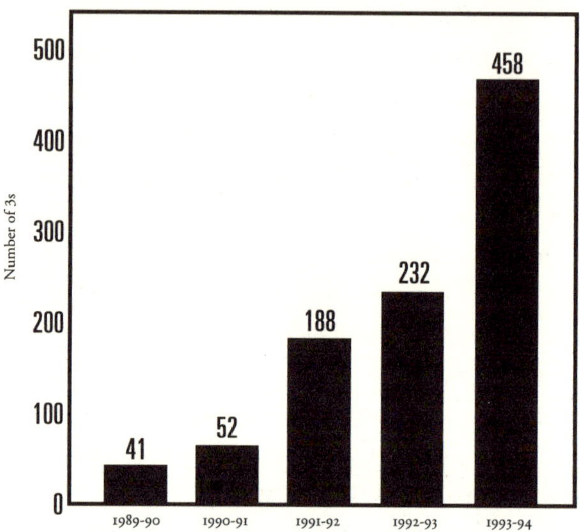

NOTE: For 1989-90 to 1992-93, test results are for only English, calculus, biology, chemistry, and physics. In 1993-94, computer science was added, and accounts for 73 exams. The AP Incentive Program began in 1990-91.

Source: The College Board

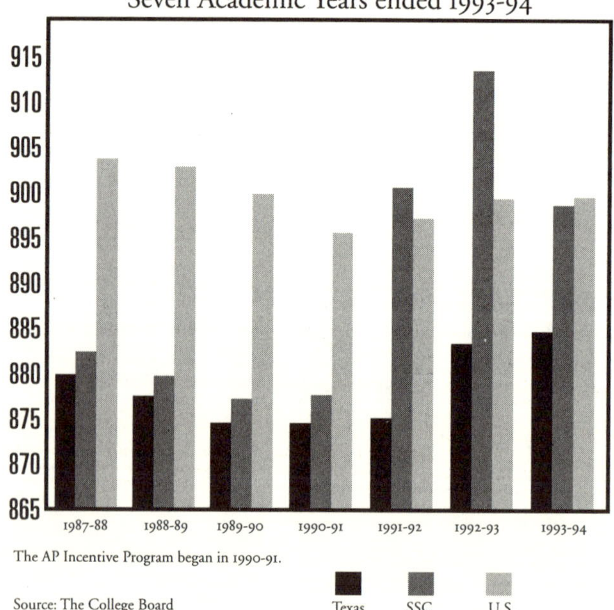

The AP Incentive Program began in 1990-91.

Source: The College Board

Duncanville, Texas, is the same as a three in Beverly Hills or Cambridge, Massachusetts.

The results have been extraordinary. In the four years of the program, an ever-increasing number of students have taken and scored three or higher on the AP exams.

The impact on overall student learning is reflected in the improved SAT scores of students whose schools participate in the program. The Super Collider is dead, but Ellis County's Advanced Placement program lives on, proof that incentives—rewards for results—have worked.

Because of these incentives, students in SSC schools now take more AP exams than U.S. and Texas students.

AP EXAMS PER 1000 JUNIORS AND SENIORS

Year	SSC Schools	Texas	U.S.
1990-91	25	52	89
1991-92	65	57	98
1992-93	95	69	106
1993-94	183	81	122

Source: The College Board

The principle of incentives for results needs to be applied across the board in our schools. A rising tide of excellence lifts all students' boats.

Incentives Work

AP Exams by discipline, academic year 1993-94

	U.S.		Texas		SSC	
	No. AP Exams	% of Exams	No. AP Exams	% of Exams	No. AP Exams	% of Exams
Math and Science	228,128	34%	9,713	29%	419	44%
English	169,464	25%	11,976	35%	436	45%
Other	286,857	42%	12,255	36%	102	11%
TOTAL	684,449	100%	33,944	100%	957	100%

Pay Great Salaries to Great Teachers

In building a new system with new responsibilities and new rewards, we must completely overhaul the way we compensate the people on the front lines—our teachers.

Today we pay our teachers as if there is no connection between teacher quality and student performance, but there is such a connection. Recent research funded by the Meadows Foundation of Dallas and conducted by Ronald Ferguson of the Kennedy School of Government at Harvard University analyzed Texas student test scores and the results of the 1986 literacy test given to all Texas teachers as part of House Bill 72. Not surprisingly, the research shows that the teachers who scored best on the literacy test produced higher test scores for their students.[5]

Enrollment in Texas schools is increasing by seventy-five thousand students every year—the equivalent of adding one Austin Independent School District to Texas every year. We need many more highly qualified teachers. To attract them, we must pay a great teacher a great salary—but notice the two "greats" in that sentence.

Right now we don't pay for greatness. We pay for survival—the number of years a teacher has been showing up for work—and the number of college degrees that teacher holds. It's a lock-step reward system that says to teachers: "Oh, you made it another year? Okay, here's a raise." The teacher may have done little that year to advance anyone's learning, but if it's time for teachers to get a raise, everybody gets one.

Remember those two second-grade teachers who were contrasted in the management reporting system discussed earlier? Under the compensation system existing in most schools, each would have been rewarded equally. That is ludicrous! We need to pay *great* teachers *great* salaries and get rid of the teachers who do not bring "value added" to a child's education.

The lockstep reward system also means we don't have enough money to pay the great ones better salaries. So every year we lose some of our best classroom teachers. Some go to law school or take jobs in major corporations just to support their families.

And because our topsy-turvy compensation system pays administrators better than teachers, many good and great teachers move up the ladder and out of the classroom in order to make ends meet. Today in most schools the average salary of an administrator is seventy percent higher than the average salary of teachers. That's the wrong incentive! It's also wrong to pay the highest salaries to coaches, as if what they do is the most important part of a youngster's education.

This lockstep reward system has got to go. Instead, we must base a significant portion of a teacher's pay on classroom performance by asking and answering this question: What improvement in academic results did the teacher achieve? The radically restructured school will provide substantial financial incentives to students and school personnel for meeting or exceeding goals.

Once we put in place an achievement-driven system, we should pay a salary sufficient for the great teacher to support a family. We can't get there overnight, but our goal should be something like $75,000 for a twelve-month contract.*

Higher salaries for teachers—yes. But there's extra responsibility to go with those higher salaries. Taxpayers will not stand for raising salaries under the same old system wherein pay raises are in large measure across the board, applying to

---

*Most teachers are paid for nine months of work. The "master teachers" who reach the top in financial rewards should work twelve months, not nine. They can help in numerous ways during the months they are not in the classroom—by training novice teachers, for example.

all teachers no matter how they perform in the classroom. We must and can differentiate among teachers based on classroom performance.

That's the only way we can move toward real accountability—which, ironically, exists only on the athletic field today.

Consider:

If a high school football coach has a losing record, he is probably going to be fired, if not this year then the next.

If an English teacher has a losing record, he gets a pay raise along with everyone else.

The difference? In sports, there is a scoreboard and a won-loss record. In other words, there are goals and clear criteria for judging the coach's performance. If the goal is to win football games, then a 2–11 record shows with glaring certainty that this coach is not getting the job done. He may be the nicest guy on earth, but he is not achieving the goal. When we put in place a system with clear, measurable goals, then each teacher in each subject will have a "scoreboard."

Those great salaries for great teachers will enable us to attract better quality students to teaching. We need them—lots of them. Tragically, we're not drawing enough of the best and the brightest to teaching anymore. If you look at the SAT scores of young people who go into teaching today compared with those who enter other fields, you see that many of our least capable graduates are headed for teaching spots. That creates a grim downward spiral as these teachers turn out another generation of poorly prepared students.

Many young people with a sense of service would rather teach than become lawyers or computer programmers, but they're scared away by the modest salaries. We can't afford to start teachers out at fifty or seventy-five thousand dollars, but if young teachers knew such rewards were possible after years of outstanding performance, that would provide a powerful incentive for them to devote their lives to students.

THOSE WHO CAN, SHOULD TEACH: THE "UNION CARD" MUST GO

Money alone won't bring us the great teachers we need. If we want more and better teachers, we must once and for all break the stranglehold of the credentialing process for teachers.

House Bill 72 opened the door to alternative certificates, and after initial resistance, some school districts have attracted qualified teachers who may not hold standard teaching certificates. But resistance remains and must be rooted out. The certificate is the equivalent of a union card in some states—you must have it to get a job. The teacher's certificate is the doorway to the field of education, and the bureaucratic watchdogs guard that door.

Does the teaching certificate guarantee great teachers? Hardly. Many good public school teachers will tell you that their teacher education courses in college were a major waste of time. Does certification even guarantee that inept teachers will not slip into the classroom? Obviously not. All of the five thousand teachers who could not pass the 1986 literacy test were properly certified.

We've all known excellent college teachers who don't hold the union card. The best private schools in our state manage to do quite well, thank you, without requiring teachers to be certified.

I have a friend who attended the University of Texas, majored in Latin and compiled a 4.0 grade point average. She has taught Latin for fifteen years in one of the finest private schools in Austin. Several years ago she contacted an urban public school district in our state and was told they could not consider hiring her unless she went back to college and took some education courses!

The union card is a bureaucratic hurdle we can no longer tolerate if our goal is to build a new school system dedicated to greatness. We've got to reach out to capable, creative people from business, industry, all walks of life.

Consider, for example, our desperate need for teachers in math and science. The most realistic way to fill this vacuum is to implore some of the best high-tech companies to loan us people who can teach some of these courses. Think how many well-qualified people at EDS, Texas Instruments, IBM, and other companies would be willing to teach a course in physics or chemistry or computer science if they were asked and their employer encouraged them to get involved.

While we're at it, think about the fine leaders from the military who might be available to teach in our schools—if they did not have to go back to college and sit through courses that teach them how to run film projectors. No institution in our country has done a better job of training a diverse work force than our armed services. It would be wonderful to watch a veteran drill sergeant from the Marine Corps teach math to seventh-grade boys! Let's turn these natural teachers loose.

You can probably think of people you know, like my friend the Latin teacher, who have mastered a skill or body of knowledge but would have no interest in getting a teaching certificate. Our kids could use their help. We can't continue a system that would not let Warren Buffet teach economics because he lacks a teaching certificate. And what if Larry McMurtry, Pulitzer Prize-winning author of *Lonesome Dove,* decided he would like to spend a few semesters teaching creative writing to high school seniors?

How would you like to be the principal who turned him down?

"Uh, sorry Mr. McMurtry, but, uh, well, you don't have the right credentials. Could you enroll in a few education courses and get that certificate?"

That's certifiably insane.

Change What Happens in the Classroom

**Encourage Experimentation,
Insist on Discipline, Teach Virtue**

Let's End the Assembly Line

Under a system that empowers principals and demands accountability, the CEOs of our schools will move to change what happens in the classroom. With the backing of the community and the school board, they'll insist that we find a new paradigm for the schools. It's about time.

For almost one hundred years we have followed the assembly-line paradigm in our schools. We organized and structured schools as if they were factories for turning out standardized products. Some factories produced shoes, others produced cars, and certain factories, called schools, produced educated kids.

As in the manufacturing world we tried to standardize our approach to education. When the school bell rang each morning we put our kids on a conveyor belt that carried them through English, math, history, and other stops on the assembly line. At each stop a skilled shop foreman poured in the facts, bolted on a few equations, tightened up a concept or two, and then sent the kids on to the next work station. At the end of the year, the finished models would roll off the assembly line and out into the world.

The industrial model always had its faults, but it made more sense half a century ago when America led the world in almost all manufacturing categories. Millions of youngsters were bound for decent-paying jobs on the assembly line. Why mess with success? Few people questioned the structure or philosophy of the schools.

Why was every model—uh, child—treated the same way? Because they had always been treated the same.

Why was each class period forty-five or fifty minutes long, with little regard for the time on task needed? Same reason.

Why was there one teacher per class? Ditto.

Why was the lesson plan the same for each child in the class, regardless of the child's learning needs? Well...

Today the Age of the Assembly Line has drawn to a close, at least in America. Look at the great cities of the Rust Belt—Chicago, Cleveland, Philadelphia, St. Louis—and you'll see the vacant hulks of factories that once employed thousands of assembly line workers. Those jobs have moved to the Philippines, Korea, and Malaysia, and they're not likely to come back.

The coming of computer technology means we can build a school model that will allow all children to learn at their own pace. Ironically, however, the assembly line lives on in our schools. With scattered exceptions, we still look to the manufacturing model when we try to educate our kids, clinging to an outdated paradigm that has left our schools stuck in a time warp.

CHANGE—OR DIE

The author Seymour Papert uses a parable to illustrate the need for breaking with the past and radically overhauling the classroom. He asks us to imagine a group of surgeons and a group of teachers from an earlier century. These time travelers have come to visit modern America, eager to see how things have changed in their respective professions.

After a century of medical progress, the surgeons would be dumbfounded in the operating room of a modern hospital:

> Although they would know an operation of some sort was being performed, and might even be able to guess at the target organ, they would in almost all cases be unable to figure out what the surgeon was trying to accomplish or what was the purpose of the many strange devices he and the surgical staff were employing. The rituals of antisepsis and anesthesia, the beeping electronics, and even the bright lights, all so familiar to television audiences, would be unfamiliar to them.

Our teachers, however, would find that little had changed in their old profession. Set them down in a modern elementary school classroom, and

> ...they might be puzzled by a few strange objects. They might notice that some standard techniques had changed—and would likely disagree among themselves about whether the changes they saw were for better or worse—but they would fully see the point of most of what was being attempted and could quite easily take over the class.[1]

As Papert notes, the driving forces of science and technology have revolutionized not just medicine but telecommunications, entertainment, transportation, and so much else. Amidst these revolutions our schools have plodded along, a Conestoga wagon on the Information Superhighway. The schools have seen a few changes—teacher aides, team teaching, and so forth—but the innovations have been slight and incremental.

Fundamentally, the system looks much as it did when Henry Ford was a young man with a big idea.

Contrast this with virtually every other endeavor in our society. Every business, every profession has had to dramatically re-engineer the way it operates or die. The changing world has offered no safe harbors. IBM, AT&T, banking, the securities industry—all have changed. One of our most lucrative and influential companies, Microsoft, did not even exist in 1980. Today Microsoft's market value exceeds that of older titans such as Chrysler and US Steel. In terms of market value added (in effect, wealth created), newcomer Microsoft ranks twelfth, ahead of much older companies such as Texaco and IBM.[2]

WHATEVER IT TAKES

To bring real change to the classroom we must allow and insist upon flexibility and experimentation. In the midst of the Depression, President Roosevelt didn't know exactly what would work to revive the crippled economy, but anyone could see that the status quo *wasn't* working. So he called for "bold, persistent experimentation" on the part of government and private industry. That should be our watchword as we transform our schools. We must let our principals experiment, to try many prospective models as we search for a winning formula.

For instance: If we have young children who are not performing at grade level, why don't we try an after-school program for them? Or how about extending the school year? Do we need a full day of school from 7 A.M. to 7 P.M.? Let's try it. Some schools have assigned first-grade students a team of teachers who remain with those students through the fifth grade. That way, the team builds cumulative knowledge of a certain child's educational needs. Likewise, we know we are not getting the job done with students who do not speak English at home. Let's try starting to educate these youngsters at age two or three.

We talked about the industrial, assembly-line paradigm that

the schools adopted long ago. In effect, that model defined education as something that everyone could get in the same way and in the same time period. But our society has other successful learning models to offer. Albert Shanker of the American Federation of Teachers believes we could borrow good ideas from a venerable teaching organization with an illustrious history: the Boy Scouts.

Consider how learning and testing take place in a Scout troop. First, there are clear-cut goals. To advance in rank, you must complete a certain number of merit badges. Some of the badges are required for everyone, but many others are optional because the system recognizes that different Scouts have different interests and abilities.

Second, there are different ways of earning the merit badges—through reading a book, interviewing an expert, working with fellow scouts, building a model, and so forth. This takes into account the different "learning styles" of Scouts learning from the Scoutmaster.

Finally, the Scout system recognizes that not all Scouts learn at the same pace. When a boy believes he is ready to advance, he announces that he is ready to be tested. One Scout may master the skills needed to get the swimming merit badge in September, while another may not be ready until May. The system sets goals and demands excellence, but has a built-in flexibility that recognizes differences in children.

Ideas like these—and countless others—might work in certain schools with certain students. What we know is that the current methods are *not* working, even after years of sporadic reform efforts. It makes no sense to continue doing the same thing that hasn't worked before. With the results we want clearly defined, we can encourage and demand an atmosphere in which our principals and teachers are free to experiment, adapt, and change, like scientists trying new hypotheses to cure a disease. The motto of our schools should be, "Whatever it takes."

GIVE PARENTS REAL CHOICE

As we said earlier, the principal is the key to academic success. There is no substitute for a first-class principal running a school. But even after we change the system, we're going to find that, occasionally, more drastic measures are needed to revive failing schools. Many of these options involve expanding real choice for families—not the bogus kind of "choice" in which students can choose Tweedledee High on the east side of town or Tweedledum High on the west side.

• One route to better schools is intradistrict choice. Why should kids be condemned to lousy schools because those schools just happen to be near their homes? If parents know that a school five miles away does a better job with math, or music, or languages, and they're willing to get their kids there in the morning, why shouldn't they be allowed to do so? In another building, maybe the emphasis is on parental involvement or phonics. Hurdles to intradistrict choice need to be knocked down.

• An even more drastic cure for bad schools may lie in breaking up huge school districts. Earlier I mentioned finding successful schools across the socioeconomic spectrum. I found great *schools*, but not great school districts or statewide systems.

That's because bigger is rarely better when it comes to education. The bigger systems get, the more problems they have. The fatter the entrenched bureaucracy, the more paperwork and procedures come between the teacher and the student.

There are no economies of scale in education. We should give serious thought to breaking up very large school districts into smaller districts organized not just geographically, but according to the varying needs of the students and desires of the parents. That would give real choice to the people who own our schools—a choice not just of buildings and location, but a choice of ideas and philosophies.

• A variation on this theme might lead to breaking up large schools into "schools within schools." Experiments are underway in Philadelphia and in New York City where two neighborhood high schools will be closed and replaced by about a dozen small ones[3]. One of the principals who takes part in our Principals' Network here in Texas has received permission to create a "school within a school" in Lubbock.

Once schools are free from the top-down tyranny of sameness, they will be able to choose the specific means-to-the-end that makes sense for them and their students. They may, for instance, adopt "ability grouping" or "homogenous grouping," as it's called, if they feel that the disparities between students are such that faster students are not being challenged, or slower students are being overwhelmed.

Likewise, some schools may want to experiment with the deliberately "old-fashioned" curricula devised by E. D. Hirsch, author of *Cultural Literacy* and *The Encyclopedia of Cultural Literacy*. According to Hirsch, most of our schools put the cart before the horse by insisting that students can develop thinking skills and reasoning skills before stocking their minds with the names, dates, events and expressions that are the building blocks of an educated mind. His study plans for the various grades emphasize the rote learning that, Hirsch and other educators believe, must precede the more sophisticated thinking and writing skills.

The point is that schools should be free to accept or reject homogeneous grouping, or Hirsch's "core knowledge" curriculum, or other educational practices, depending on what seems right for certain students at certain times. Flexibility is the key. Let a hundred flowers bloom—and a thousand ideas and techniques be pursued by teachers who are free to be the professionals they set out to be.

Charter Schools Can Provide Real Choice

Likewise, let's expand choice by experimenting with a dramatic departure from the old top-down, pyramid-shaped system discussed in the last chapter. If a principal fails to produce results over a given period of time (perhaps three years), it may be time to put the school up for bid as a "charter school."

Eleven states now permit the creation of charter schools (see Appendix, page 165) whereby school districts enter into a contract with a third party to operate a particular school. That third party might be

- a group of teachers,
- a principal who wants to put in place a new type of school,
- a for-profit company such as Educational Alternatives, Inc., which recently contracted with school districts in Baltimore and Hartford, Connecticut,
- a good corporate citizen like IBM, EDS, or Texas Instruments that might be willing to take over the management of an existing school or create a new public school at their place of business, open to children of all of their employees,
- a nonprofit entity that has devoted itself to helping kids and is willing to expand its services. In the Dallas–Fort Worth area, for example, the Salesmanship Club has worked for years with at-risk kids in a wilderness environment, while Dallas Can! Academy has helped hundreds of potential dropouts earn the GED. Either group might want to form a charter school.

The charter school's contract has to free the school from the process-driven rules and regulations that force the sameness of our schools. In exchange for that freedom, the managers of the charter school must operate with the same amount of money the school has been spending, take all comers as public schools do, and be accountable for academic improvement and meeting academic goals. If they don't, they lose their charter after an agreed-upon period of time.

The objective of all these programs—charter schools, school within schools, and so forth—should be to give real choices to parents to meet the individual educational needs of their children.

The Voucher System Will Not Save Our Schools

I believe strongly that charter schools are the best way to bring competition and market forces into the public school system. Those who advocate a private-school voucher system say that vouchers will do the same thing by granting families a state-issued check that can be used to offset costs of education in a private school. But while charter schools will foster competition *within* the public school system and thus strengthen it, the voucher system will in the long run weaken our system without accomplishing the goal of a first-rate educational opportunity for all kids. In fact, the voucher system will not solve the problems of the public schools—and if adopted, vouchers will lead to the ruin of our private school system.

In the first place, there simply aren't enough private schools to absorb any significant percentage of the children that public schools must educate. The National Center for Education Statistics tells us that in 1993, in the entire country, only 5.4 million students were enrolled in private schools, a number the Center predicts will grow to 6.2 million by 2003.[4]

We have more than 3.6 million students in Texas public schools alone, and will have almost a half million more by the year 2000. Even assuming that the number of private schools doubled, the vast majority of Texas kids will remain dependent upon public schools for their education.

Second, the fundamental problem in public schools is the lack of political will to change the system. You can't run away from the problem with private school vouchers. If we do not stand and fight the political battle to win, I guarantee that those vouchers, like almost all government assistance, will come with strings attached—requirements that will ruin the private school system. If the state is helping to pay, the state will want a say.

For example, before issuing vouchers, the state would undoubtedly require private schools to hire only certified teachers and use state-approved textbooks. You can bet other rules and regulations would soon strangle the private schools the same way they have strangled the public schools.

INSIST ON DISCIPLINE

Today in too many schools, metal detectors are becoming more prevalent than merry-go-rounds or slides. Texas teachers are increasingly confronted with abusive and/or violent behavior.

In a recent survey conducted by the Texas Federation of Teachers, thirty-five percent of respondents said there was a "significant problem" with student discipline or misbehavior in their classroom, and a much larger group, eighty-three percent, said such problems were common elsewhere in the school—halls, cafeteria, and so forth. Almost thirty-six percent had been

Texas Federation of Teachers Survey

Abusive or profane language by students to classmates	82%
Failure to do assigned homework	78%
Unexcused absences	66%
Vandalism of school property	66%
Threats of physical violence to students	63%
Theft	63%
Unexcused tardiness	61%
Assault on students	53%
Students in the halls during class	53%
Racial tension	40%
Student gangs	39%
Drug abuse	37%
Forgery of hall passes, excuses, etc.	36%
Abusive or profane language by students to teachers	36%
Threats of physical violence to teachers	17%
Other	15%
Assault on a teacher	8%
None of the above is a problem at school	3%

NOTE: Totals do not equal 100 percent because teachers could check more than one item.

Source: Texas Federation of Teachers, Dallas Morning News, June 11, 1993

the target of abusive or profane language by students, while seventeen percent had been threatened with physical violence and seven percent had been attacked.

This situation is intolerable. For too long we have concerned ourselves with the rights of a few disruptive children and ignored the rights of all children to a safe and secure environment in which learning can flourish. Where there is no order, there will be no learning.

Of course the classroom does not exist in isolation from the world outside. Our increasingly violent campuses are a microcosm of a violent society. In 1992, one violent crime referral was made to a Texas juvenile probation department every seventy-three minutes. These included:

- one homicide referral every twenty-eight hours,
- one sexual assault referral every six hours,
- one robbery referral every four hours, and
- one aggravated assault referral every three hours.

In 1994 the Texas attorney general revealed that approximately 120,000 juveniles were arrested in Texas in 1993, but the state has only about two thousand juvenile detention beds. The average juvenile criminal racks up six felony referrals before spending any time in a state facility.

This dramatic rise in juvenile crime is dramatically illustrated by the changes in juvenile commitments between 1973 and 1993. (See chart next page.)

Nationally the statistics are equally grim. A 1991 National Institute of Justice survey of students in ten inner-city public schools found that twenty-two percent of students reported owning a gun, a third of whom said they carried a gun to school "regularly or occasionally."[5] According to *American Educator* magazine, thirty-six percent of inner-city junior high teachers

Changes in Juvenile Crime
As reflected in Texas Youth Commission
commitments for 1973 and 1993.

1973	1993
• Predominant offenses were theft at 48.7 percent and disobedience at 27.2 percent.	• 34 percent of commitments were for violent offenses.
• 8.9 percent of youths were admitted for alcohol or drug violations.	• 31 percent had 5 or more felony referrals (arrests) prior to commitment.
• 4.9 percent were committed for violent offenses.	• 80 percent had used alcohol or drugs; 49 percent are chemically dependent.

Source: Texas Youth Commission
Austin American Statesman

report they have been threatened by a student. Eleven percent of suburban and seven percent of rural teachers say they have been threatened. Extensive surveys of teachers who have left the profession reveal that most often, working conditions—not salary—were cited as the reason for quitting.[6]

The Texas Federation of Teachers is pushing for a "zero tolerance" policy for the violation of rules and regulations that permit learning to take place. That approach will be debated by the Texas Legislature in its 1995 session.

Here again we must decentralize, pushing authority and decision-making power down to the schools and into the classrooms. Every child has a right to an education, but *no child has the right to prevent others from learning*. The teacher knows when a child is disrupting class and violating the rights of others, and the teacher must have the absolute right to remove that child from the classroom. Further, the principal must have the absolute right to remove that disruptive youngster from the school.

But we all know what happens when teachers and principals try to deal with threats to the learning environment. The first time a lawyer calls the superintendent and threatens to sue because a youngster was expelled, the school board must have the courage to hold firm and politely (or otherwise, as far as I am concerned) tell the lawyer to go sue. The state should back up school personnel with indemnities against liability and cover legal costs. As it stands now, many principals and teachers are afraid to confront disruptive students, fearing they might be held personally liable in a lawsuit filed by an angry parent.

Violent and disruptive students must lose their rights to an education in the setting of the regular classroom. However, we can't simply expel them to the streets where they may become more deeply mired in crime and violence. States and local districts should make alternative arrangements—separate schools, boot camps, work camps, and so forth—where these troubled youngsters can earn the right to reenter the regular classroom. Costs for those programs could be absorbed through the juvenile justice system.

THE SCHOOL MUST MEET THE NEEDS OF THE CHILDREN

There is no magic wand we can wave to solve the problems of violence, drugs, teenage pregnancy, and broken families. Everyone agrees that the best foundation for any child is a happy home in which both parents love and support the child, but the reality is that many children do not have such homes. In fact, according to some recent statistics, the "Leave It to Beaver" two-parent home of the fifties is a distant dream.

In light of these grim facts, it's discouraging to hear so many teachers say that "parental involvement" is an absolute requirement for a child to succeed in school. If that's the case, folks, then the battle is already lost. In the first place, let's be honest: In Dallas County last year, more than two thousand babies were born with cocaine or other drugs in their bloodstreams.[7] Do we really want parents like that involved with our schools?

We must all work to reduce violence, poverty and neglect, but if we say that our public schools cannot succeed until those problems are solved, we will lose another huge portion of the young generation. Over the past ten years, seventy-three percent of the increase in the school age population of Texas has come from households at or below the federal poverty level. According to TEA data, forty-seven percent of Texas students are now eligible to participate in the federal school lunch program.[8]

So we must play the hand we are dealt, realizing that, like it or not, the schools in many instances must do without parental involvement and still do whatever is necessary to educate these children. We must rid ourselves of the 1950s notion that the schools merely supplement the learning and nurturing that happens in the home. In all too many cases, the child is not getting intellectual and emotional support at home; if it doesn't happen at school, it doesn't happen.

That's why many of our schools must become the central delivery point for existing social services such as immunizations, counseling for child abuse, adult literacy classes, and more. The idea makes sense for a couple of reasons. For one, it will cut down on the time children spend shuffling from one place to another while their parents seek these services. Why not bring the service to those who need it, rather than putting a child with an upset stomach on a two-hour bus ride to the county hospital? For another, it will actually cost us less money if we consolidate many of these services in one place.

I am not saying that teachers should become caseworkers or that the school day should become a series of doctors' visits and group therapy sessions. What I am saying is this: In the past, our schools didn't require much of our students. The schools we need will demand much more. We must adopt high standards, set clear goals, and demand that our students achieve. But in turn we must invest more in them. An abused child with an empty stomach doesn't care about the causes of the Civil War. He's worried about the causes of the war in his home each night.

REMEMBER: VIRTUE MATTERS

There's something else we can do to help our kids and help our society. The mounting problems of teenage pregnancy, random violence and juvenile crime have awakened us to the fact that we've failed to address something crucial in our children's education. Call it virtue, moral character, ethics—by whatever name, it's vital to civil society. So why are our schools so silent about it?

Our failure to cultivate virtue in our children—and honor it in our society—sends its own kind of moral message. When we allow youngsters to violate rules and suffer no consequences, we are communicating something about the moral standards we accept. When parents and their lawyers threaten suits against principals who try to keep order, and the school backs down, that speaks volumes about our priorities.

One reason we have been silent about virtues is that in our society, we usually associate those matters with religious belief. Nobody wants a return to the old days when churches and schools were almost interchangeable, but we have gone to such extremes that teachers can't even discuss the Bible, much less universally accepted moral codes such as the Golden Rule. It's time to recognize that the framers of our Constitution were concerned with freedom *of* religion, not freedom *from* religion.

I am not talking about teaching Christian doctrines or Jewish doctrines, or the Methodist view or the Catholic view or the Buddhist view or the Islamic view. But reaching across the spectrum of religions and denominations, there are certain virtues we can all agree on, among them

- respect for the individual
- the conviction that all of us have rights *and* responsibilities
- prudence
- justice
- fortitude
- citizenship

- courage
- obedience to laws
- hard work
- faith
- tolerance for the views and diversity of others

We cannot continue to be so skittish about religion that we treat it as a poison gas—let a little of it get out in the classroom, and all is lost. For one thing, forbidding the mention of religion distorts the history our young people should learn. It's simply not accurate to describe the Pilgrims, as one textbook does, as "people who made a long trip." Students can't really understand Dr. Martin Luther King as a civil rights leader without discussing the central role that his personal faith, and that of the black and white church community, played in the success of the movement. We can teach *about* religion without teaching a particular religion.

Whatever their religious beliefs, students should know that religion, along with technology, mobility, war, the legacy of slavery and other forces, has shaped our country and our culture. Faith was important to the founders of this country, though they certainly disagreed about the particulars of religious denominations. Great men and women have been motivated by their faith. Teaching English literature or Western civilization while ignoring the powerful influence of religious belief is like teaching astronomy without mentioning the sun.

We can't look at the depressing evidence of violence, illegitimacy, and despair in our society without realizing that something has gone terribly wrong. While our teachers should never favor any particular religion or denomination, our schools have a legitimate role to play in arresting the decline of citizenship and morality that we're suffering. Besides learning how to read, write, and count, our students must learn how to live. Our schools must help them.

CHAPTER 8

OVERHAUL OUR SCHOOL FINANCE SYSTEM

IF WE PUT MORE MONEY INTO THE SAME OLD SYSTEM, WE WILL GET THE SAME OLD RESULTS

The problems of our schools are many and complex, but for years policymakers in Austin have answered them with two simple words: More money. It's a rare politician who can resist throwing money at a problem. We've thrown and thrown. Here are the results.

- Since 1975–76 Texas public school budgets have grown from $3.4 billion to $18.9 billion for the 1993–94 school year.[1]
- This increase in spending averaged about ten percent compounded per year.
- This amounts to $5,248.52 per student for operating expenses, debt service and capital outlays.[2]

This increase in spending has had a dramatic impact on homeowners. According to the Texas Research League, the statewide average school tax on a $80,000 homestead has

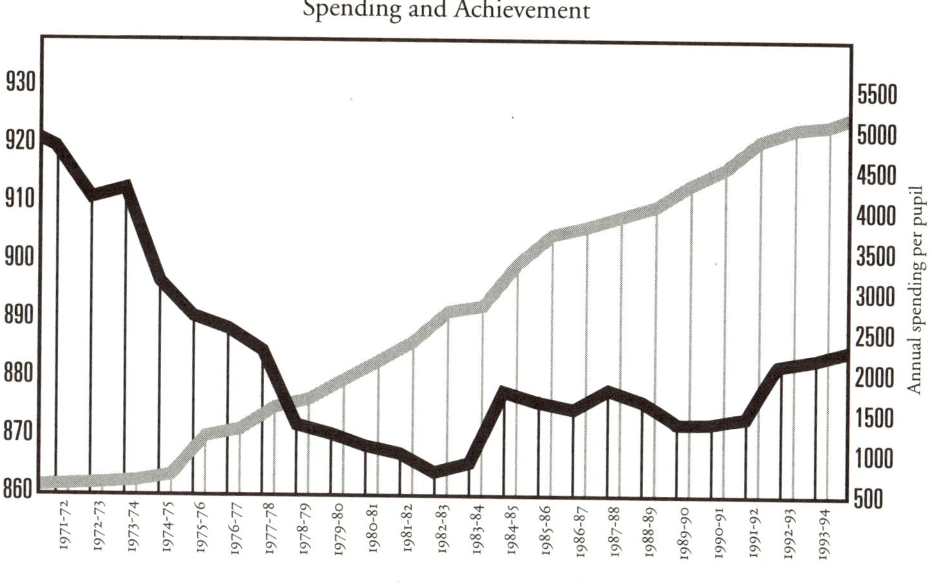

increased from $430 in 1983–84 to $962 in 1993–94. In Dallas the school tax on that $80,000 homestead has risen from $372 to $947; in Houston, the number has climbed from $263 to $781.[3]

Looking at those figures, it wouldn't be fair to say that Texans have been miserly with their schools. But as vividly demonstrated by the chart above, Texas taxpayers and parents did not get their money's worth.

So we've thrown more dollars than Nolan Ryan has fastballs. And we're not alone. Nationally, between 1970 and 1990,

• Real per-pupil expenditures increased eighty percent from $3,000 to $5,400 in 1992 dollars.[4]

• During those two decades, American schools reduced the average pupil-teacher ratio from 23.2 to 17.2.[5]

• The percentage of teachers with master's degrees rose from less than 2.5 percent in 1961 to more than 50 percent by 1986.[6]

But across the country, performance on the National

Performance and Spending
Total Elementary and Secondary School
Expenditures vs. SAT Scores

• While expenditures on elementary and secondary education have increased more than 200 percent since 1960, SAT scores have declined 73 points.

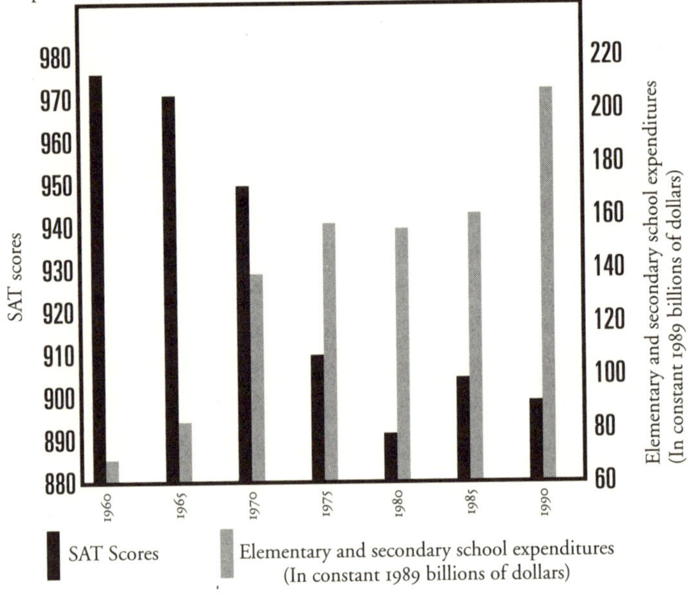

Source: The College Board and U.S. Department of Education

Assessment of Education Progress has essentially remained flat since 1970, while the level of education required to survive in the twenty-first century economy rises every year.

In Texas as elsewhere, the answer is clear: We cannot spend our way to greatness. If we could, we would long ago have made it to the promised land.

Is money irrelevant to quality of education? Absolutely not. As we've discussed, excellent teachers and principals who are truly CEOs of their schools will deserve more money, not less. We will need to spend more money on education to produce the results we want. We will need to lengthen the school day and the school year, and of course that will require more money. Eventually money will be part of the answer.

But not now. Not until we transform our schools so that the

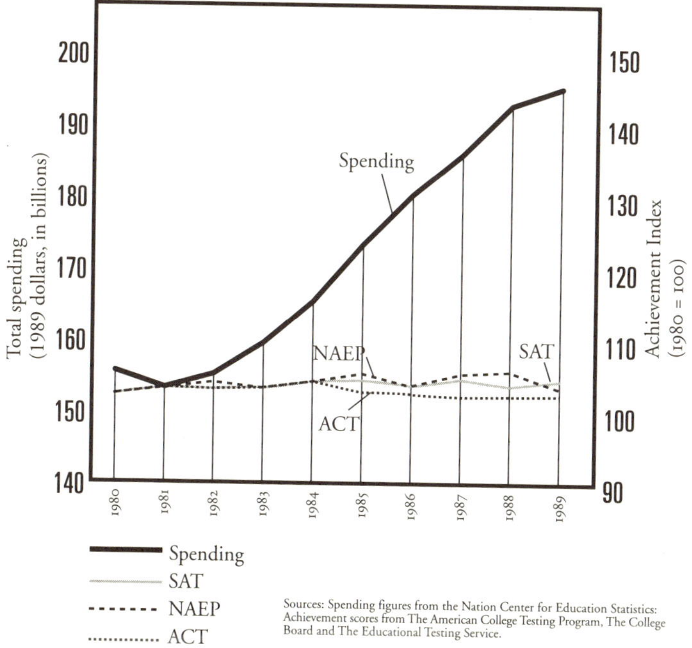

money can be effectively and efficiently spent. We should lengthen the school day, yes—but if we increase spending in order to do that now, without changing what happens in the classroom, that extra money would just be wasted.

Spending more on the system we have now would be akin to spending more to increase the output of an assembly line that's making defective products. If you just hire more workers for a company that is making substandard batteries, you will have more people cranking them out and the work may go faster, but at the end of the day you will only have a bigger pile of substandard batteries.

To justify more money for the system as it is now, we would have to trace its problems to a lack of money. It is my firm conviction, as I've made clear in these pages, that insufficient funding is not the major cause of our broken system.

Unfortunately, our state policymakers have spent the past five years operating on the assumption that the real problem *is* lack of money, so they have reduced everything to one question: "Where can we get additional funds to equalize state aid to education?" As they have struggled over "Robin Hood" and "Son of Robin Hood," few lawmakers were asking the right questions: "How can we change our school system to produce better academic results?" "What new results will taxpayers get for their investment?"

While we've spent years fighting the Robin Hood school funding wars, we have failed to face the core problem of our school finance system. The real problem is not "rich" districts or "poor" districts. The real problem is threefold.

First, our spending patterns, regardless of how much money is in the system, make no sense. We reward failure rather than success and have no material incentives to encourage excellence. Second, the state is failing in its responsibility to provide the funds to ensure that every youngster can get the education he or she needs. Third, we do not spend our money wisely. For example, in 1993–94, barely half of the public school employees statewide were classroom teachers. More than forty percent of the amount budgeted for current operations statewide was for activities outside the classroom. Administrative salaries averaged almost seventy percent more than the average for classroom teachers.[7]

WHY THE SYSTEM BROKE DOWN

Following America's victory in World War II, as our soldiers came home determined to build a better life, the need for improved education was on everybody's mind. Through the G.I. Bill, Congress provided the opportunity for returning veterans to receive a college education. Here in Texas, state leaders began to confront the deficiencies in our public school system.

In 1949, the Texas legislature responded to the call for better education by passing the first statewide reform of our public school system, the Gilmer-Aiken law. One of the major provisions of the bill recognized the state's duty to provide education. In the words of the Texas Constitution, "…it shall be the duty of the legislature of the state to establish and make suitable provisions for the support and maintenance of an efficient system of public free schools."[8] The state increased its share of school funding to about seventy-five percent, with local school districts supplying the rest.[9]

For many years after Gilmer-Aiken was passed, the state continued to provide the majority of the funds needed to give everyone an education. Of course there were disparities in the wealth of various school districts across the state, but when the state was paying the bulk of the cost of an education, those disparities did not prevent the districts from providing the constitutionally mandated education for all.

All was well until the state eventually defaulted on its obligations to the students of Texas. Slowly, the percentage the state provided for education began to decline as more and more of the burden was shifted to local districts. When Texas suffered the economic downturn of the 1980s and state tax revenues failed to grow as they had in the boom times of the 1970s, the percentage supplied by the state slid from close to seventy-five percent to its current low of forty-five percent.

That led to the *Edgewood v. Kirby* case, in which a school district in San Antonio sued the state. Eventually the case landed before the Texas Supreme Court, which in 1989 issued a decision that shook Texas to its foundations.

When the state supplies less than half the cost of an education, the court said, and the local districts have only one way to make up the deficit—local property taxes—the great differences in property tax wealth among the districts make it impossible to provide all youngsters an equal opportunity for a first-rate education. Children in poor districts were not getting an even break, the court held. The system was declared unconstitutional. The state would have to find another way to fund the schools.

There were two ways the state could have responded to the court ruling. We could have bitten the bullet, increased the state's share of the education pie, and taken the emphasis off local property taxes. Or we could have taken the other road and faced one of two choices: Equalize all schools down to mediocrity or equalize them up to excellence.

Unfortunately, we chose the down-to-mediocrity approach. Instead of restoring the state's share of funding to previous levels, we have spent years in a bitter struggle to reallocate local funds, devising formulas by which we could take money from one district and send it to a poorer district to make things "equal." The Texas Supreme Court ruled in January, 1995 that this revised system was constitutional. Well, it may be constitutional, but it is a system that provides everyone an equally mediocre education.

Designing a fair system that will lead us to excellence does not require a genius—but it does take political courage.

How to Fix the Funding System

First, we must decide what kind of education we want for our young people. We must spell out clearly what they should know and be able to do. We can't develop a fair and efficient school finance system until we know what kind of results we want. If we don't know—well, as the Cheshire cat said to Alice in Wonderland, when you don't know where you're going, any path will take you there.

The previous chapters outline the steps we must take to design a new system committed to high standards, anchored to clear goals and driven by real accountability for results. Then, after we have decided where we are trying to go, we should determine how much it should cost to provide that type of education.

Keep in mind that we are talking about what kind of basic academic education a high school graduate needs to survive and thrive in the twenty-first century. In determining that cost, we must be honest with ourselves: the state cannot assume responsibility for everything we might want. This is not Utopia. We should not include the cost of providing football programs or home economics or administrators. The state's priority must be what happens in the *classroom*, not in the driver education cars or on the football field.

Once we determine the price of providing that basic education, the state should pledge to provide seventy-five percent of that cost. Local school districts would make up the remaining twenty-five percent of that basic package, plus anything else a district believes would enhance the basics.

For instance, if a local school wants to provide three foreign languages instead of two, it would be free to do so, but it would have to pay the extra costs. Local schools would also have to decide which electives and extracurricular activities they want to provide over and above the basic academic education. If the local community wants to foot the bill for, say, journalism classes or more Astroturf football fields, it would be free to do so—at its cost. The local districts would also be free to decide how many administrators they need, and how to pay for them. (Of course, that task will be easier if we truly decentralize, for then we will be able to slash administrative costs considerably.)

In a perfect world we could afford everything for our students, and the bills would be paid by some infinitely wealthy benefactor who takes joy in writing checks. But in the real world choices will have to be made. Even after the state increases its share of the education budget, we still won't be able to give everyone a Mercedes—but we can be sure that nobody has to walk.

The system I am advocating has a number of healthy byproducts. For one thing, it will foster more community involvement in the schools. Today, the average citizen knows little about what the schools spend and why. Under the new system, a school will say to the community, "we want to hire a journalism teacher, build a new field house, and increase the salary of two administrators. Here is what it will cost you, the taxpayers, to do these things." Community involvement will be enhanced when taxpayers know they must bear the cost of these choices.

To complete the revolution, the state's seventy-five percent share of the education costs would be distributed on a per-child basis to each campus. If the cost of giving each child a basic education is, say, $4,500, then a campus in Laredo and a campus in Houston would each receive seventy-five percent of that figure—$3,375 for each child enrolled. The local districts would then understand that they will have to make hard choices about the extras they consider worth paying for.

Then we need to pass a constitutional amendment that defines the state's obligation as we have defined it—to provide seventy-five percent of the cost of that basic academic education. That will permanantly get the courts out of the schools and allow us to focus on the classroom.

But we cannot stop there if we want an efficient and excellent system. In addition to the basic allotment, we need to put significant funding into a reward system that will provide big dollars to those districts that show the most improvement—improvement we'll be able to measure once we put the other segments of the new system into place. As we discussed in Chapter 6, we now give schools more money if they are not getting the job done. We need to reverse that and give financial incentives to the schools that are succeeding.

HOW TO PAY FOR THE NEW SYSTEM—WITHOUT AN INCOME TAX

If the Legislature will adopt this plan or a similar plan, the court will be satisfied. Even more important, our school leaders will be able to win back taxpayers' confidence with a new "contract'" that spells out how their money is being spent and what results they will get for their money.

At that point, I for one am quite happy to engage in a debate about tax policy. Leadership requires nothing less. If additional revenue is needed, I am willing to go to bat for it. The important thing is for the state to assume its responsibility to provide the lion's share of a quality education for every youngster.

Let's assume that after we determine what kind of school system we want, we decide that a solid education should cost $4,500 dollars per child. Remember, this money will only cover the classroom costs of providing our basic education.

To reach the goal of the state funding seventy-five percent of this basic cost, I would increase the state's share of the education pie five percent per year for six years.

Should there be a shortfall between available revenue and the cost of this plan, here are several solutions that do *not* involve an income tax.

1. Reduce state spending in lower priority areas.

Included in the Appendix on page 167 is a list of agencies and programs I would favor eliminating if more funding is needed for our schools. If we truly believe education should be our number one priority, we must act accordingly.

2. Reallocate current tax revenue.

We could change the way we spend the gasoline tax we

pay today. Currently twenty-five percent of that tax per gallon goes to public education and seventy-five percent goes to build highways.

We could change that allocation to a fifty-fifty split and generate $1 billion more for education in the next biennium. Highway funding would not greatly suffer; the Transportation Bill passed in the 1992 session of Congress should make up the shortfall. Besides, when it comes to priorities, are roads more important than our children's education?

These two approaches may very well eliminate the need for a tax increase. If not, it does not there are plenty of alternatives that would not involve the creation of a personal income tax.

3. Tax Increases

For instance, we could increase the percentage rate applicable to the current sales tax by 1%. This would generate another $3.2 billion for the biennial budget. We could eliminate most of the current sales tax exemptions (except for food and medicine) and raise $4.6 billion for the biennial budget. Or we could tax services as well as goods and raise an additional $4.6 billion.

And there are other alternatives. We could tax commercial property at the state level not only to gain revenue at the state level, but to assure an equitable tax base at the local level.

And keep in mind, increasing the state's share of education spending should permit a reduction of local property taxes.

Of course there is no way of knowing just how much money we need until we have a plan, but these funding methods show that *we do not need an income tax to solve our education crisis.*

We must not settle for a constitutional system. We must strive for a school finance system that produces excellence.

We have the opportunity, if we have the will, to put in place a system that will let us be the best we can be, compete and win in the world economy, maintain our high standard of living and control our own destiny.

As we have seen, this plan pushes decision-making down to the local level, to the people who live with the consequences of the spending decisions. It involves taxpayers in deciding how their money is spent and increases the number of people who feel they have a stake in the schools.

As important as it is for the taxpayers to help set priorities for spending, there are many other ways that we must all get involved in saving the schools. Let's look at some of those ways.

CHAPTER 9

WHAT YOU CAN DO NOW TO SAVE OUR SCHOOLS

I remember a conversation I had back in 1984 when we were fighting to pass House Bill 72. I was talking with two typical officials of one of the state's education associations. Determined to preserve the status quo, they were beseeching me to water down one of the many changes we had proposed.

One of them looked me in the eye and said, "Young man, even if you win in the legislature, a year from now you will be gone and we will go back to doing what we were doing before you came along."

They sounded pretty confident, these guardians of the status quo, and no wonder. They knew the difference between *talking* change and making change happen.

Believe it or not, the easy part is deciding what needs to be done to transform our schools. Changing a large private institution is hard enough—just ask IBM. But the difficulty of the task increases geometrically when you are talking about a public institution that is immersed in the political arena and is encrusted with layer after layer of special interest groups clinging like barnacles. The fight to change our schools is not a hundred-yard dash, it is a marathon.

The administrators I mentioned above were confident they would prevail. Eventually these pesky reformers would have to go back to their real lives and jobs. The publicity would die down, the camera crews would go away, the editorial writers would turn their attention to another crisis. School would let out for the summer (after all, the kids have to go home and help harvest the crops!) and it would be business as usual.

That means business as usually conducted by the pressure groups I've called the Iron Triangle (see Chapter 2)—the Texas Education Agency, the various education organizations, and the staff of the legislature. They're used to making education policy themselves. Too often real people—the customers and taxpayers who support the system—are not heard from.

THE POWER OF ONE

I don't want to make the task of breaking the Iron Triangle's grip sound easy, but it is possible for people, even small groups of people, to have an impact on education policy if they're willing to get involved.

I will never forget how I learned that lesson. When we were working hard to pass House Bill 72, I was personally calling on every single legislator, explaining what was in the bill and why, and asking for their help, their support and above all their vote. I was particularly intent on persuading one Central Texas legislator who carried plenty of weight with his fellow lawmakers and was a fierce floor debater.

Unfortunately, every time I came to his office he had just heard from another education trade association that was out to scuttle the bill.

The teacher associations were incensed because the bill would require their members to demonstrate their competency.

The superintendents were mad because of all this talk about accountability and assessment and so on.

The football coaches were opposed to the whole bill and especially to the "no pass, no play" provisions because, as more than one told me, "If you don't let them boys play football, they will just rob gasoline stations."

As a result, this key legislator told me almost every day that he just didn't see how he could support the bill when all these groups were opposed to it. They had mailing lists of voters in his district. They knew how to bring pressure to bear on him at home.

It looked bad, but I kept going back and pleading my case. One day he said to me, "Well, it looks like you won't take no for an answer."

I told him that was certainly my objective.

The legislator shook his head and said: "Okay, I'll make a deal with you. I'll vote in accordance with the mail from my district."

I muttered to myself that this was not exactly the kind of leadership I had in mind, but if that was the best I could do, I would hope for the best.

A week later, the morning before the bill was to come to a floor vote, I went back to his office and asked whether he was going to support the bill. Much to my relief, the answer was yes!

I expressed my gratitude. Then I just had to ask about the mail count from his district. What kind of outpouring had he seen from his voters?

"One letter for and none against!" he replied, beaming.

Here we were after months of statewide media attention focused on this issue, in the final days of a special session devoted only to education, and this legislator had heard from every education trade group, but only one *person* from his district.

I still have that letter framed on the wall in my office at home. It reminds me that in a democracy, we get what we deserve. And what we're willing to work for.

JUST FOR THE KIDS

As I've traveled our state over the past few years, talking about the problems of our schools, so many people have asked me the same question: "What can I do? How can I get involved?" It's a question that deserves an answer.

We know that the myriad interest groups are always at work in Austin, haunting the halls of the capitol, slapping backs and counting noses. Every group that lives off the system has some kind of full-time representative in Austin looking out for its interests. When they need to weigh in on a bill affecting their members, they know who to call and where to send the faxes.

Superintendents, principals, coaches, teachers, special education teachers, school nurses, counselors, textbook suppliers…. There's just one group left out: Our children. Who speaks for them?

To match the tenacity of the special-interest lobbyists, we must put someone at that table who is always thinking of what is in the best interests of the children, to ensure that their voices are heard when education policy is made. The power of one can be great, but the power of many is even greater. To increase our impact and truly transform our schools, we need to band together.

That's why I have started a nonprofit foundation called Just for the Kids to promote the agenda in this book. (See page 117.) The voice of Just for the Kids will be as loud as you decide to make it. If we can show the policymakers that thousands of Texans care and demand to be heard, our impact will be great.

Those administrators I told you about earlier were counting on me to get frustrated and go away. Well, they were wrong. I haven't gone away. And we can't go away. Our kids deserve better. But it will take all of us to change this system.

As we have seen, transforming our schools will require changes from the bottom up—on individual campuses and in classrooms—and from the top down, with action to set goals and measure progress. Working individually and through the collective power of Just for the Kids, you and I must fight the political battles necessary to put our plan in place and keep it there.

What will Just for the Kids do? Many things.

• Build a solid local membership base by recruiting members from all across the state, from every geographical area and every part of the socioeconomic spectrum, so that political leaders will know that we care and that we know what decisions they are making.

• Engage in direct-mail campaigns to people in their homes, and buy radio spots and newspaper ads to recruit new supporters for our crusade.

• Demand and receive a seat at the table when policy is made and implemented. That way, we can counter the special interest groups.

• Broaden our base by forming coalitions with other organizations such as the Texas Business and Education Coalition, chambers of commerce, individual businesses interested in transforming education, and local grassroots organizations like the IAF organizations led by Ernie Cortes.

• Monitor progress in transforming our schools. We will analyze the mountains of reports and data available and let you know how the schools are doing. If a local school district begins to weaken in its resolve to change, we will let you know so you can let them know to stand firm.

• Support real change agents within the school districts. We will find the guerrillas in the system—principals and teachers who are winning the battle today against long odds—and we will support them and protect them against the backlash from the system.

With your help, Just for the Kids will be the lobbyist for the schoolchildren of Texas. I hope you'll decide to join me in this quest to transform our schools. Let's give our kids a voice. In the meantime, let's talk about the steps each of us can take to rebuild our schools.

If you agree with the agenda for transforming our schools outlined in this book, please join with us by calling 1-800-762-4645 and becoming a member of Just for the Kids. The annual membership fee is $35. As a member, you will receive a newsletter that will keep you informed about education issues all over the state and will alert you when your voice needs to be heard on behalf of the schoolchildren of Texas.

WHAT STUDENTS MUST DO

Let's start with the responsibilities that our students have for their education. First, students must understand that we as a society owe each of them the *opportunity* to get an education. The rest is up to them.

Inherent in that responsibility is the obligation to treat with respect those professionals who give their time and their knowledge to students. In our transformed school system, there is no place for anyone who verbally or physically threatens or abuses a teacher.

Second, our students must understand that they will have to work harder. Education is not something that is *done to* a young person; it's an active process that requires teamwork and commitment from both student and teacher. Transforming our schools will mean new attitudes about responsibility, and that starts with rethinking the time students spend in school.

It's no wonder our students fare poorly when measured against students from other countries; their foreign competitors spend considerably more time in school. This chart graphically illustrates the point:

BEHIND THE WORLD IN 180 DAYS

Country	Days Spent in School
China	251
Japan	243
West Germany	226-240
South Korea	220
Israel	216
Luxembourg	216
Russia	211
Netherlands	200
Scotland	200
Thailand	200
England/Wales	192
Hungary	192
Swaziland	191
Finland	190
New Zealand	190
Nigeria	190
France	185
Ireland	184
Spain	180
Sweden	180
U.S.A.	180[1]

As economist Lester Thurow of MIT says in the book, *Where We Stand*, "Americans think they can learn in 180 days what the rest of the world takes 220 to 240 days to learn."[2]

Alas, we're wrong. We can't. And we lose even more ground because the longer summer vacation means that our elementary school teachers have to spend four to six weeks of each new school year reteaching what the students forgot during June, July, and August.

It does not take a professional educator or a rocket scientist to quickly see why the Japanese and South Koreans always fare better than American students in international competition. Why wouldn't they, when longer school days and a longer school year permit Japanese elementary school kids to spend fifty-two percent more hours in the classroom than American children? In middle school and high school the gap widens to sixty percent.

By the time a Japanese student finishes the twelfth grade, she has easily put in the equivalent of four more years of education than her American counterpart. And the gap is even wider when you take into account that approximately half of all Japanese students spend an average of five extra hours a week in private tutoring. Despite all this evidence, our school systems have been slow to lengthen the school year or school day.

THE "H" WORD

You *can* go home again, and we can and must go back to the days when homework was not only assigned but graded. Today only twenty-seven percent of our thirteen-year olds spend two or more hours a day on homework while seventy-three percent spend three or more hours watching television. By the time they graduate from high school, American students have spent two thousand more hours in front of the television than in school.[3]

The "homework gap" between our students and the Japanese is enormous. In primary school, Japanese students

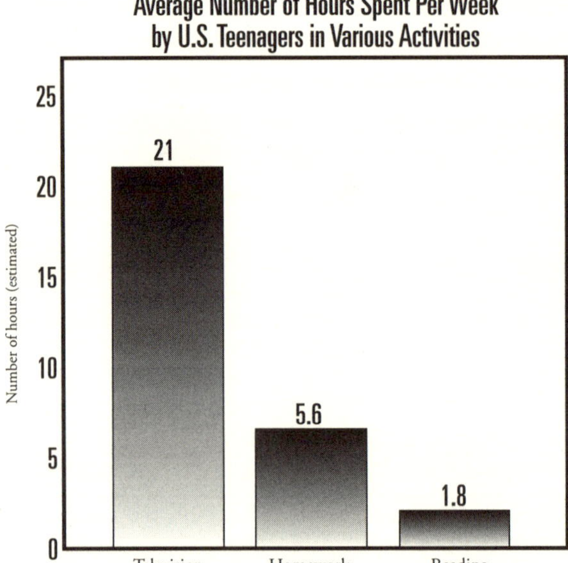

Source: The Index of Leading Cultural Indicators

spend 8.3 hours a week studying while Americans spend just 1.8 hours hitting the books. In middle school the gap grows to 16.2 hours versus 3.2 hours; in high school, 19 hours versus 3.8 hours. If you count homework and classroom time as equal, a Japanese high school graduate actually spends 22.3 "years" in academic work, compared to the 12 years an American student spends. ̄

I don't want to duplicate the Japanese system in America. But what if we played the Japanese in a Little League World Series and found that the Japanese team practiced twice as much as the American team? Would you be surprised at the winner?

Too Little Time on Task

Even when our students are in school, they don't spend enough time actually working on important subjects. A recent Carnegie Corporation study revealed that U.S. high school students spend an average of only three hours every school day on core academic subjects. In the typical American school, students spend just forty-one percent of the day on English, math, science, history, geography, foreign languages, civics, and fine arts.[4]

Contrast the time on task in U.S. schools with our international competitors.

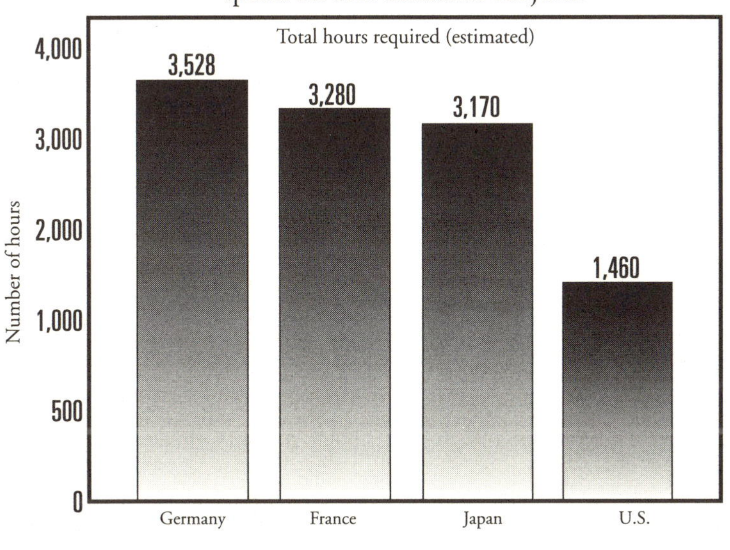

Source: Newsweek

In the transformed school system we seek, students will have to work harder and take responsibility for their actions.

WHAT PARENTS MUST DO

Three things:

1. Get involved.
2. Stay involved.
3. Don't expect getting involved to be easy.

"Children's success is very dependent on how actively involved their parents are," says Dr. Barbara Schneider, a senior social scientist at the University of Chicago. "When parents are involved in school they give their children a sense of community, of having a system of shared values and standards."[5]

Thirty years ago researchers at the University of Chicago documented that the more parents valued education, the better their children did in school. Since then study after study has demonstrated that, regardless of socioeconomic background, students whose parents are involved in their education enjoy increased motivation, have higher test scores, and get better grades. Parents benefit as well from involvement. They feel better about themselves, they get along better with children and they become more involved in other community programs.[6]

All that sounds great, and most schools today pay lip service to the ideal of parental involvement. It's one of those good things everybody is for, at least in theory. But when parents show up ready to get involved, school officials don't always know how to accommodate them.

The sad truth is that in many schools, the prevailing culture sees parents as potential problems to be managed, preferably at arm's length. After all, involved parents may ask a lot of specific questions and demand answers. They might want to know, for instance, why an inept teacher who had lost control of his class was not being replaced.

An example of this "No Parents, Please—We're Educators" mind-set showed up recently when officials at a primary school in Queens painted a red line on the sidewalk just outside the school's front door. Parents were told they could not cross the line to enter the building, not even to drop off or pick up their children.

TAKING RESPONSIBILITY FOR YOUR CHILD'S EDUCATION

Today, with site-based management the law of Texas, it's important that parents of school children be willing to serve on school-based councils—although these councils should never try to usurp the principal's day-to-day decision-making power. And of course there are other ways to be part of the life of the school—attending school events, going to parent-teacher conferences, volunteering to help classroom teachers, and asking specific questions: How can I help my child? How can I help you teach my child? Don't be afraid to hold the administrators' feet to the fire. Demand that they focus their creativity on academic improvement.

If you think about it, both teachers and parents often forget one vital fact: You, the parent, have been teaching this child ever since he or she was born. Nobody knows that child better than you do. You probably know something very important about how to motivate the child and help him learn. Now you must establish a partnership with your child's teachers and principal to continue that education.

If you're lucky, your school will make it easy for you to get involved. But whether it's hard or easy, you must get involved and stay involved. And that means taking your child's education as seriously as you demand he or she take it.

Do you have a homework policy? Do you have a television policy? In too many homes, children can hardly be blamed for not studying amidst the noise of stereos, "Monday Night Football" and "Home Improvement." To help families get back to the basics, the Reverend Jesse Jackson and a group of African-American church leaders are distributing pledge cards urging parents to take their children to school, meet their teachers, read their report cards, and turn off the televisions for at least three hours every night. (See Appendix, page 168.)

But failure to provide a good study atmosphere is not a "black thing" or a problem confined to low- and moderate-income households. In many affluent homes, there are simply too many televisions, Walkmen, video games, and other electronic distractions. Kids are great at spotting hypocrisy. If parents fill the house with television noise and show that they're indifferent to books and ideas, they shouldn't expect their kids to develop a great love for Shakespeare and George Orwell.

You must monitor your child's academic progress and you must be the advocate for your child. Providing learning opportunities outside of school, such as visits to museums, concerts, and historical sites, is a must for parents who value their children's education.

Third and certainly not last, you must become part of the transformation of your school because education is truly too important to leave to the educators. You must carry the banner for the changes presented in this book. Because our current system is badly broken, it's not enough to stress education at home and not be involved at school. If the schools do not adapt to the twenty-first century, your efforts—our efforts—will be for naught.

This book, like Just for the Kids, is designed to help you become an advocate for change. If you have the courage to ask a campus principal or a school board to list their specific, measurable goals, and reveal the plan by which they will meet those goals, that will force those in charge to deal with these important issues. They may not even *have* any specific, measurable goals—but if they know you're not going away, they'll probably do their darnedest to come up with some! Never be afraid to ask: "Where is the plan? How do we measure our progress?"

There is another reason parents must speak out. It's the nature of the system that people in charge seldom hear from anyone who is not defending the status quo. In turn, school officials tend to defend the status quo and say things are getting better. Or they respond to groups demanding group benefits by telling how many minority teachers they have hired and how much money they are spending in this or that part of town—as if any of that tells us what the kids are learning. The Texas Business and Education Coalition has published an excellent brochure setting out what you should expect from your schools and giving suggestions about what you should ask. I have included a copy in the Appendix on pages 169–170.

Finally, here is perhaps the most important thing parents can do to help their kids in school: Back the school's efforts to maintain an orderly, disciplined environment. Support the teachers. Tell your child you expect him to learn from those teachers.

REACHING OUT TO PARENTS

During the years that my children were going through public schools, I never once had a teacher, principal, or counselor send home anything that spelled out what I should do to help my children perform better in school. Parents Night once a year is not enough. If schools really want parental involvement, they shouldn't simply assume that parents know what to do; they should tell them at the beginning of the school year what they can do to help. Would they like for parents to review each night's homework? Would they prefer that parents *not* help with certain types of homework?

Parents might start by demanding that schools make it easier to communicate with teachers. In the mid-nineties, in the middle of a communications revolution, why are teachers trotting off to the teachers' lounge to get in line for the telephone? Why don't all teachers have phones in their rooms with voice mail? Today, many American families have personal computers at home. Why don't we link teachers and parents through electronic mail?

WHAT BUSINESS MUST DO

Many progressive business people have long known that there are at least two good reasons for getting involved in education: a sense of social responsibility, and a healthy dose of self-interest. As noted earlier, we cannot have a healthy business climate without a first-class school system to provide the qualified workers of tomorrow.

So we've seen a developing relationship between business and the schools. All over the state, businesses are helping students by providing tutors, contributing computers, and helping to raise money for the schools. All this is to the good and should be applauded, but it won't transform our schools.

To a large extent, many of the business-school partnerships have been little more than "feel good" programs: Give the A students a banquet, hand out some corporate-sponsor T-shirts, and see you next year. Good students deserve at least some of the recognition we usually reserve for athletes, but if that's all that business does with the schools, the result will be incremental change at best. We need more.

For one thing, most business-school partnerships lack an outcome analysis. In forming its contract with the school, the business must ask hard questions of itself and of the school.

What results do we want from this program?

How will we measure those results?

Have we improved student learning?

Likewise, business must be ready to withdraw its support if there is no increase in academic results over time. The School Performance Management Analysis discussed earlier can and should be duplicated in every district. Without the discipline of an outcome analysis—which any successful business already does with its other functions—millions of dollars and hours are wasted each year.

To return to the Pony Express analogy we used earlier, too many business-school partnerships do little more than provide lighter saddles and tastier oats for the horses. Business must give the highest priority to forcing systemic reform—transforming our schools. Without this priority, the system will swallow up the efforts of individual businesses. Those Pony Express riders will keep galloping along toward mediocrity.

And just as the power of one can be multiplied by Just for the Kids, the efforts of individual employers can be multiplied if you will join reform groups like the Texas Business and Education Coalition (TBEC).

The TBEC, a coalition of reform-minded educators and business leaders from across the state, supports

- development of community-based coalitions to encourage reform,
- creation of comprehensive systems of accountability for both student achievement and management efficiency for all schools,
- implementation of campus-based management of schools,
- challenging curricula and course requirements,
- preparing and retaining effective educators,
- delivering community health and social services intended for children at school campuses,
- expansion of early childhood programs.

To join in these efforts in your home town and help deliver the message to our state government leaders, call TBEC at (512)480–8232 or write to Texas Business and Education Coalition, 400 West 15th, Suite 910, Austin, TX 78701.

PUTTING PRESSURE ON THE SCHOOLS

Businesses must band together to demand systemic, step-by-step, radical overhaul as a condition of their support of the schools. Local school boards must hear this message from business:

"Show us specific, measurable goals and a plan to accomplish the goals. Show us how you will measure progress toward the goals. Show us a system that will reward results and insist on consequences for failure. Give us a plan for a disciplined, drug-free learning environment. Until we see a plan that will transform the system, the business community will not support increased taxes or bond issues for the schools."

Business cannot be afraid to speak out. Of course speaking out can be controversial. It may embroil your company in local school politics. But do you really have a choice? Right now, business carries more than half of the local property tax burden. If business leaders do not fight for systemic change, that burden will keep increasing. If you don't fight for real change, where will you find the qualified employees who will help you compete and win in the worldwide economy?

Will you import them from Japan? A few years ago the CEO of IBM revealed that sixty-seven percent of seven hundred manufacturing employees the company had tested could read only at a sixth-grade level or lower. If things go on as they are, how much will you have to spend in basic remedial education within your company in order to get qualified employees?

If a business really wants to have a dramatic impact on the schools, the best and quickest way to do so is to help train principals for their new responsibilities in site-based management. Under the existing system, principals are being given more autonomy; under the transformed system I advocate in this book, they would have much more as the real CEOs of their schools.

But they're not being trained in the uses of their new power. Today's successful principals do not succeed because of the training they have received. They learn from trial and error, or they instinctively understand how to recruit, evaluate, retain, motivate, and reward their teachers and other staff members.

Businesses today spend millions to train their own leaders in these very skills. Opening these training opportunities to school principals in the summers could have a great impact because principals today are in desperate need of more leadership training as opposed to curriculum development. Our principals also need help in budgeting as well as skills in building teamwork. Business can help with all of this and in so doing, help to transform the schools.

Even without spending any money, business can also have a large impact on standards and expectations. All teachers know that one of the keys to motivating students is to help them see that what they do in school matters outside of school. How can business help get that message across? First, when employing young people for summer or after-school jobs, business owners and personnel departments should give first priority to those students who enrolled in and passed advanced placement tests. Striving for excellence should be rewarded.

Second, when permanent jobs are offered to high school graduates, every prospective employer should ask for the applicant's high school transcript. A student with a B average should be hired before a student with a C average. That will help young people see that school is not a closed loop, but is connected with the outside world. If McDonald's would hire after-school workers based on grades, believe me, the word would quickly spread.

BEYOND THE BUZZWORDS: WHAT POLITICAL LEADERS CAN DO

If our political leaders really want to help in transforming the schools, they must first go beyond the buzzwords that tend to substitute for real action.

Today "change" has become the favorite message of every political consultant—and thus of every candidate. But while "change" sounds great in a sound bite, chanting the slogan over and over does not produce meaningful change. Transforming the schools will require leadership from men and women who possess vision and courage, and something less flashy but still vital: Stamina, the stick-to-itiveness that will see us through the long fight and determine whether or not we are successful.

My travels across the state have convinced me that the people are ready for real change and are anxiously awaiting leaders who will lead the charge. The reason is clear. Many of us sense that the American dream is slipping away. We're anxious and angry. We want someone to speak the truth in clear language and tell us where we stand. We want a leader who will set forth a clear and realistic vision of where we are, where we are going, how we will get there, and how we will pay for it.

But our leaders have not gotten the message. Instead they persist with the tired old techniques of telling us we can have Utopia without any kind of sacrifice. *Nobody will have to change for change to occur; nobody will have to work harder or reach higher. No, the only thing you need do is vote against my stupid, backward, dishonest, conniving opponent and everything will be fine. Promise.*

People are sick of this partisan bickering, and nowhere is it more counterproductive and more destructive than in our discussions of education. More than any other state issue, education must be free of partisan politics. We must focus only on what works for kids. What works is not liberal or conservative but common sense.

Voters today yearn to hear a discussion of the common good—if politicians would give it to them. They've had it with a political debate that plays off one narrow group against another, exploiting our differences and ignoring our common interests. People want to be public-spirited and accept responsibility. They're waiting for the leaders who will show them the way.

They're also waiting for leaders who might, once in a while, talk about why our public schools matter. They must explain why the public education system affects each and every one of us, whether or not we have kids in public schools.

Meaningful change cannot occur in the current, poisoned political environment in which 1) leaders are afraid to tell the truth, 2) demagogues try to destroy anyone who thinks "outside the box" with unorthodox solutions, and 3) winning the next election is seen as the only thing that matters.

Our leaders must be willing to put hard issues on the table. For instance, when discussing accountability in education, we must say in plain language that it is too hard to fire incompetent teachers and principals who are cheating our kids. Some of the teachers' and principals' groups may not like that, but it's the truth. We have to speak those uncomfortable truths and be willing to take the heat. Losing an election is not the worst thing that can happen to a leader. The worse thing is to run a campaign based on empty promises and half-truths, telling voters that things will be fine if we just buy some nice new deck chairs for the *Titanic*.

Today our state leaders must step forward and level with people: The job we are doing today, despite the good intentions of many in our school system, is not good enough for what lies ahead in the twenty-first century, when today's seventh-graders graduate from high school.

Our leaders must lay out a plan of what our twenty-first-century school system will look like and give us a plan for getting there. They must be truthful; we won't get there overnight and we won't get there without sacrifice and perseverance. They will challenge us all—students, parents, business leaders, taxpayers—to do our part.

Above all, our leaders must now function as mediators between an angry, confused electorate and the education establishment that has been slow to heed the voters' wishes. They must say to the citizens, "Don't give up on the schools. We can fix them and make you proud again." And to the educators they must say, "The voters will no longer support this tired old system. Let's make a new contract with the taxpayers."

If we all do our parts, I know that we can transform public education and save our schools for the children of our state. I'm in this fight to stay. I hope you'll join me.

Notes

Chapter 1: A State Still at Risk

1. National Commission on Excellence in Education. 1983. *A Nation at Risk: the Imperative For Educational Reform.* Washington, DC: U.S. Department of Education.

2. Sharp, John. 1993. "Introducing the Texas 100." *Fiscal Notes.* October. pp. 10–11 and, Texas Research League. 1994. *Benchmarks: 1993–94 School District Budgets in Texas.*

Chapter 2: How Bad Are Our Schools?

1. Brooks, A. Phillips. 1994. "TEA Says Schools Are Improving But 'A Long Journey' Remains Ahead". *The Dallas Morning News.* August 3.

2. *Report Card on American Education 1994: A State-by-State Analysis.* 1994. Washington, DC: American Legislative Exchange Council. September 9.

3. Texas Education Agency. *Final Campus Accountability Rating.* Unpublished report, September 1, 1994.

4. Ibid.

5. Texas Higher Education Coordinating Board. 1994. *Third Annual Report on the Effectiveness of Remediation.*

6. National Center for Education Statistics. 1994. *The Nation's Report Card.* Washington, D.C.: Office of Educational Research and Improvement, U.S. Department of Education.

7. Ibid.

8. Texas Research League, 1991.

9. Simon, Janice. 1994. "Most Advanced Jobs Will Need Advanced Training By 2000," *Galveston Daily News.* July 24.

10. National Commission on Children. 1991. *Beyond Rhetoric: A New American Agenda for Children and Families: Final Report.* Washington, D.C. The National Commission on Children.

11. Ibid.

12. Shanker, Albert. 1988. *"State of Our Union" Address Before the American Federation of Teachers*. San Francisco, California. July 2.

13. *Report Card On American Education 1994:* A State by State Analysis.

14. "Texas Means Business." *Professional Review*, Fall 1994. pp. 36-40.

Chapter 3: Why We Must Save the Schools—Now

3. Sharp, John. 1994. *Forces of Change: Shaping the Future of Texas*. Austin: Office of the Texas Comptroller of Public Accounts.

4. Texas Department of Commerce.

Chapter 4: Decide on the Results We Want

1. Goodwin, Doris Kearns. 1994. *No Ordinary Time: Franklin and Eleanor Roosevelt; The Home Front in World War II*. New York: Simon and Schuster.

2. Kennedy, John F. 1961. Special message to a joint session of Congress, May 25. *Public Papers of the Presidents of the United States: John F. Kennedy*. pp. 404, 405.

3. National Education Goals Panel. 1994. *The National Education Goals Report*. Washington, D.C.

4. Mirel, Jeffrey and Angus, David. "High Standards for All." American Educator, Fall 1994. p. 41.

5. Hancock, Lynell. 1994. " In Defiance of Darwin: How a Public School in the Bronx Turns Dropouts into Scholars." *Newsweek*, October 24. p. 61.

6. Smothers, Ronald. 1994. "To Raise the Performance of Minorities, A College Increases Its Standards." *The New York Times*, June 29. p. A 11.

7. Frady, Marshall. "Profiles: Outsider." *The New Yorker*. 67:52. February 17, 1992. pp. 39–69.

8. Sharp, John. 1994. *Forces of Change: Shaping the Future of Texas*.

9. Manno, Bruno V. 1994. "Outcome Based Education: Miracle Cure or Plague?" *Hudson Briefing Paper: Shaping the Future*. 165 (June).

9. Ibid.

Chapter 5: Give Authority to Those Responsible for Results

1. Sirota and Alpe Associates, Inc. 1984. *TEA Pilot District Management Process Survey: Statewide Results.*

2. Select Committee On Public Education. 1984. *Review of Teacher Perceptions of Paperwork Requirements.*

Chapter 6: Measure and Reward Results

1. Bissenger, H. G. 1990. *Friday Night Lights: a Town, a Team, and a Dream.* Reading, MA: Addison-Wesley Publishing Company.

2. *Forces of Change*

3. Comptroller of Public Accounts, Research Division. October 18, 1994

4. Lyndon B. Johnson School of Public Affairs. 1993. *A Decade of Change: Public Education Reform in Texas, 1981–1992: Special Project Report.* Austin: Lyndon B. Johnson School of Public Affairs and Texas Education Agency.

5. Ferguson, Ronald F. 1991. "Paying For Education: New Evidence on How and Why Money Matters." *Harvard Journal on Legislation.* Vol. 28: 465–498.

Chapter 7: Change What Happens in the Classroom

1. Papert, Seymour. 1993. *The Children's Machine: Rethinking School in the Age of the Computer.* New York: Basic Books, Inc.

2. "The Forbes 500." *Forbes.* April 25, 1994.

3. Chira, Susan. 1993. "Is Smaller Better? Educators Now Say Yes for High School." *New York Times*, July 14. p. A1.

4. National Center For Education Statistics. 1994. *The Nation's Report Card.* Washington, D.C.: Office of Educational Research and Improvement, U.S. Department of Education.

5. League of Women Voters Education Fund. 1993? *Juvenile Violence and the Juvenile Justice System in Texas.* Austin, TX: League of Women Voters.

6. "Teachers Who Quit Often Cite Work Conditions, Poll Says." *The Dallas Morning News.* September 18, 1994.

7. Parkland Hospital. Telephone interview with Karen Hanratty, November 4, 1994.

8. Texas Education Agency. 1993. *Snapshot '93: 1992–93 School District Profiles.* Austin: TEA Office of Policy Planning and Evaluation.

Chapter 8: Overhaul Our School Finance System

1. Texas Research League. 1994. *Benchmarks: 1993–94 School District Budgets in Texas.* Austin: Texas Research League.

2. Ibid.

3. Ibid.

4. *Report Card on American Education 1994: A State-by-State Analysis.*

5. Ibid.

6. Ibid.

7. *Benchmarks.*

8. Constitution of the State of Texas; Article VII, Section 3I.

9. *Report Card on American Education 1994: A State by State Analysis.*

Chapter 9: What You Can Do Now to Save Our Schools

1. Bennett, William J. 1994. *The Index of Leading Cultural Indicators: Facts and Figures on the State of American Society.* New York: Simon and Schuster.

2. Wolfe, Michael. 1992. *Where We Stand: Can America Make It in the Global Race for Wealth and Happiness?* New York: Bantam.

3. *Index of Leading Cultural Indicators*

4. *Washington Post* Weekly Edition, May 16–22, 1994.

5. Schneider, Barbara and James S. Coleman, eds. 1993. *Parents, Their Children, and Schools.* Boulder, CO: Westview Press.

6. Ibid.

APPENDICES

Law and Policy Changes in the 1980s
State Level (1980-1990)

• High school graduation requirements	42 states raised standards.
• Student testing	Momentum from '70s carried forward; 47 statewide programs by 1990.
• Accountability	Widespread adoption of measurement and indicator systems; by 1990, 23 states go beyond test scores and use an integrated set of indicators.
• Teacher standards	Sweeping changes, particularly in teacher testing, from a handful of states in 1980 to 39 in 1990 that require passing a test to enter teacher education or being teaching.

School level (1984-1988)   **Percentage of high schools**

School level (1984-1988)	Percentage of high schools
• Stricter attendance standards	73%
• Set academic requirements for athletics and extracurricular activities	70%
• Stricter conduct standards	70%
• Longer school day	40%
• More homework	27%
• Higher teacher pay	23%
• Longer school year	17%

SOURCE: Educational Testing Service and Dallas Morning News

Partial List of Educational Associations

Association of Texas Professional Educators
Texas Association of Community Schools (TACCS)
Texas Association of Non-Public Schools
Texas Association of Private Schools
Texas Association of Public School Employees
Texas Association of School Administrators
Texas Association of School Business Officials
Texas Association of Secondary School Principals
Texas Classroom Teachers Association
Texas Congress of Parents and Teachers
Texas Cooperative Education Association
Texas Elementary Principals and Supervisors Association
Texas Faculty Association
Texas High School Coaches Association
Texas Industrial Vocational Association (TIVA)
Texas Music Educators Association
Texas State Teachers Association
Vocational Agriculture Teachers Association of Texas
Texas Retired Teachers Association
American Federation of Teachers
Dallas Alliance of Black School Educators
Texas Council for the Social Studies
Texas Association of School Boards
Texas Association of Suburban Schools
American Association of Physics Teachers, Texas Chapter
American Association of Bandmasters
Texas Educational Secretaries Association
Vocational Home Economics Teachers Association of Texas
Texas Association of Distributive Education Clubs of America
Texas Driver and Traffic Safety Education Association
Texas Home Economics Association
Texas Joint Council of Teachers of English
Texas School Public Relations Association
Texas Vocational Technical Association

Dropout Results
1992-93 School Year

	Total 7-12th Enrolled	Total Dropouts	Change From Previous Yr.
African American	202,708	8,538	-832
Hispanic	481,771	23,531	-1,789
White	726,247	15,345	-2,400
Other	37,297	885	-100
Total	1,448,022	48,299	-5,122

3 Year Trend
Dropout

	1989-90	1992-93	Change
Total	70,040	48,299	-21,741
African-American	13,012	8,538	-4,474
Hispanic	30,857	23,531	-7,326
White	24,854	15,345	-9,509
Other	1,317	885	-432

Source: Texas Education Agency

SAT/ACT/PSAT
1994 Results

1993 and 1994 SAT, ACT and PSAT/NMSQT Summary Results

| | 1993 | | 1994 | | Change: 1993-94 | |
	National	Texas	National	Texas	National	Texas
Mean SAT Scores						
Verbal	424	413	423	412	-1	-1
Math	478	472	479	474	1	2
Total	902	885	902	886	0	1
Mean ACT Scores						
English	20.3	19.7	20.3	19.7	0.0	0.0
Math	20.1	19.9	20.2	19.9	0.1	0.0
Composite	20.7	20.1	20.8	20.2	0.1	0.1
SAT:						
Number Tested	1,044,465	82,537	1,050,386	83,963	5,921	1,426
% Graduates Tested*	43%	45%	42%	48%	-1%	3%
ACT:						
Number Tested	875,603	54,115	891,714	56,735	16,111	2,620
% Graduates Tested*	36%	30%	36%	32%	0%	2%

	Fall 1992	Fall 1993	Change: 1992-93
PSAT/NMSQT Juniors - Mean Scores:			
Verbal	39.5	40.1	0.6
Math	45.0	45.5	0.5

Sources of data in table: College Board; American College Testing, Inc.

Table prepared by Texas Education Agency, Office of Policy Planning and Evaluation.

*Graduate numbers used to determine percentages based on College Board report of Western Interstate Commission for Higher Education projections. This information includes both public and private school students.

Selected High School Course Enrollments
Fall 1991 vs. Fall 1993

	October 91	October 93	Percent Change
Total HS Enrollment	889,388	927,209	+4.3%

Course Title	October 91	October 93	Percent Change
English			
• English I	212,386	277,267	+30.6%
• English II	184,621	231,887	+25.7%
• English III	166,925	201,186	+20.6%
• English IV (includes English-Academic)	143,196	163,917	+14.5%
Mathematics			
• Algebra I	221,142	352,764	+59.6%
• Geometry	142,829	170,323	+19.3%
• Algebra II	113,178	131,369	+16.1%
Science			
• Physics I	28,072	33,971	+21.1%
• Biology I	204,238	266,344	+30.5%
• Biology II	15,054	17,114	+13.7%
• Chemistry I	93,100	111,899	+20.2%
• Chemistry II	5,351	5,703	+6.6%
Social Studies			
• U.S. History	244,559	254,324	+4.0%
• World History Studies	163,013	176,648	+8.4%
• World Geography	73,628	95,770	+30.1%
Second Language			
• Spanish			
• Spanish I	118,614	142,926	+20.5%
• Spanish II	83,734	96,540	+15.3%
• Spanish III	11,414	15,478	+35.7%

Accountability Rating Standards for 1994

	Exemplary*	Recognized*	Accredited/ Acceptable	Accredited Warned/ Low-performing
Base Indicators				
Spring 1994 TAAS Reading Writing Mathematics	at least 90% passing each subject area (all students and all student groups)**	at least 65% passing each subject area (all students and all student groups)**	at least 25% passing each subject area (all students)	below 25% passing any subject area (all students)
1992-93 Dropout Rate	1% or less (all students and each student group)**	3.5% or less (all students and each student group)**	no 1994 requirements	no 1994 requirements
1992-93 Attendance Rate	at least 94% (grades 1-12)	at least 94% (grades 1-12)	no 1994 requirements	no 1994 requirements
Additional Requirements				
Sustained Performance	must meet for each TAAS subject area (all students and each student group)**	not applicable	not applicable	not applicable
Required Improvement	not applicable	must meet for each TAAS subject area below 90% passing (all students and each student group)**	must meet for each TAAS subject area with less than 25% passing (all students)	did not meet for each subject area with less than 25% passing (all students)

*A district cannot be rated Exemplary or Recognized if it has one or more low-performing campuses
**Student groups are African American, Hispanic, White, and Economically Disadvantaged.

National Goals for Education

Readiness
Goal 1: By the year 2000 all children will start school ready to learn.

School Completion
Goal 2: By the year 2000, the high school graduation rate will increase to at least 90 percent.

Student Achievement and Citizenship
Goal 3: By the year 2000, all students will leave grades 4, 8, and 12 having demonstrated competency over challenging subject matter including English, Mathematics, Science, Foreign Languages, Civics and Government, Economics, Art, History, and Geography. Every school in America will ensure that all students learn to use their minds well, so they may be prepared for responsible citizenship, further learning, and productive employment.

Teacher Education and Professional Development
Goal 4: By the year 2000, the nation's teaching force will have access to programs for the continued improvement of their professional skills and an opportunity to acquire the knowledge and skills needed to instruct and prepare all American students for the next century.

Mathematics and Science
Goal 5: By the year 2000, United States students will be first in the world in Mathematics and Science achievement.

Adult Literacy and Lifelong Learning
Goal 6: By the year 2000, every adult American will be literate and will possess the knowledge and skills necessary to compete in a global economy and exercise the rights and responsibilities of citizenship.

Safe, Disciplined, and Alcohol and Drug-Free Schools
Goal 7: By the year 2000, every school in the United States will be free of drugs, violence, and the unauthorized presence of firearms and alcohol, and will offer a disciplined environment conducive to learning.

Parental Participation
Goal 8: By the year 2000, every school will promote partnerships that will increase parental involvement and participation in promoting the social, emotional, and academic growth of children.

State of Texas
1994 School Report Card

The School Report Card gives you important information about your child's school. The report provides information on student academic performance, school finances, student and teacher characteristics and student enrollment. For middle schools and high schools it may also show the dropout rate and performance on the SAT and/or ACT. As you read it, remember that every school is different with its own special strengths and needs. For that reason, the report card cannot tell you everything. The Texas Education Agency urges you to find out more about your school from its teachers and principal; and we encourage you to stay actively involved in your child's education.

L.R. Meno,
Commissioner of Education

Report for: Sample H S
of the Sample ISD

Principal: Dr. Al Johnson
Total Enrollment: 1,748
Grade Span: 9-12

Accountability Rating: Acceptable
A school may be rated Exemplary, Recognized, Acceptable, or Low-performing.

Produced by Policy Planning and Technology Services Texas Education Agency

State of Texas 1994 Report Card
Sample High School
Sample ISD

Student Performance

The TAAS (Texas Assessment of Academic Skills Test) is a standardized test that students in grades, 3, 4, 5, 6, 7, 8, and 10 must take. The TAAS has tests in Reading Math, and Writing. The graph shows what percent of students passed each subject of the TAAS.

The table shows what percent of all students passed each subject of the TAAS. It shows the percent who passed in the state, the district, the school group and the school. Two years are given for the school. The school "Group" is a group of 100 other Texas schools that are similar to this school.

*TAAS Percent Passing for Grade 7

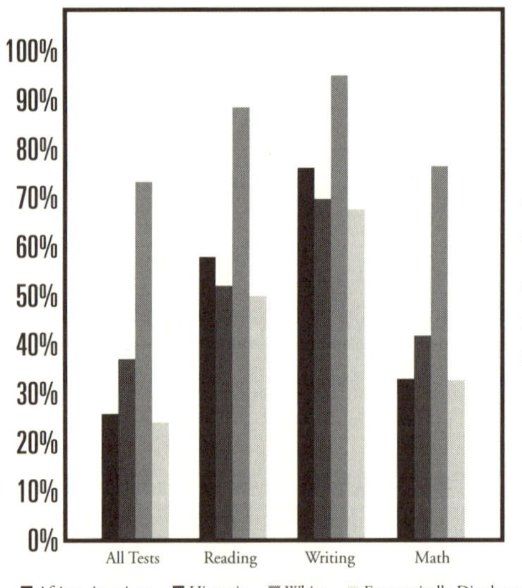

All Students

	All Tests	Reading	Writing	Math
School (1993)	49.7%	68.7%	82.3%	57.7%
School (1992)	45.5%	70.2%	76.6%	53.7%
Group (1993)	55.1%	77.6%	85.9%	60.6%
District (1993)	38.4%	65.4%	75.2%	45.4%
State (1993)	54.4%	76.4%	83.2%	60.7%

*The goal of the state is to have at least 90% of the students pass each subject of the TAAS. Schools that have fewer than 25% of their students passing may be rated "Low-performing." The accountability rating for the school is given on the first page of the School Report Card.

State of Texas 1994 Report Card
Sample High School
Sample ISD

TAAS Percent Passing for Grade 8

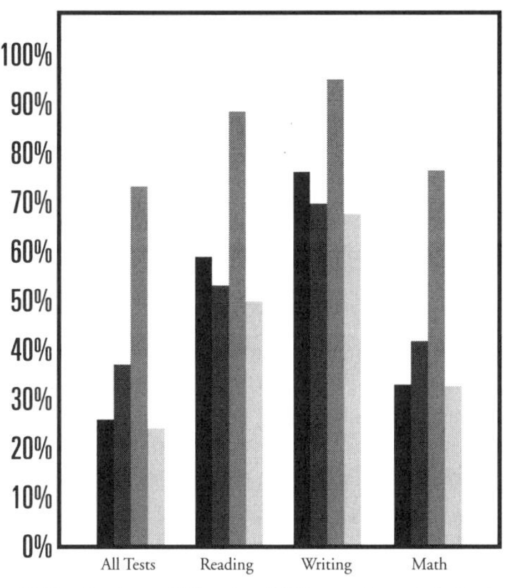

All Students

	All Tests	Reading	Writing	Math
School (1993)	49.7%	68.7%	82.3%	57.7%
School (1992)	45.5%	70.2%	76.6%	53.7%
Group (1993)	55.1%	77.6%	85.9%	60.6%
District (1993)	38.4%	65.4%	75.2%	45.4%
State (1993)	54.4%	76.4%	83.2%	60.7%

TAAS Percent Passing for Grade 10

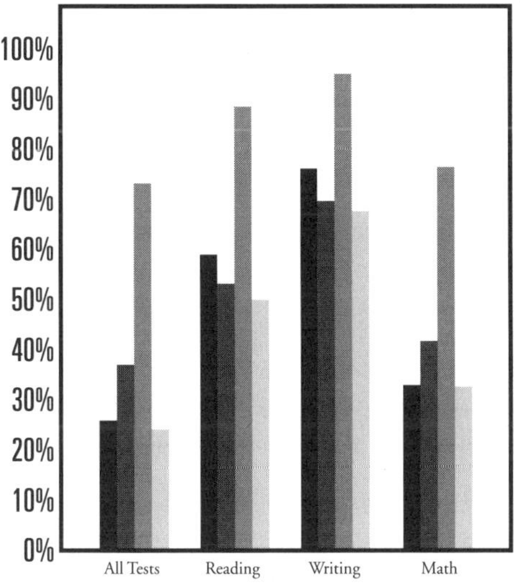

All Students

	All Tests	Reading	Writing	Math
School (1993)	49.7%	68.7%	82.3%	57.7%
School (1992)	45.5%	70.2%	76.6%	53.7%
Group (1993)	55.1%	77.6%	85.9%	60.6%
District (1993)	38.4%	65.4%	75.2%	45.4%
State (1993)	54.4%	76.4%	83.2%	60.7%

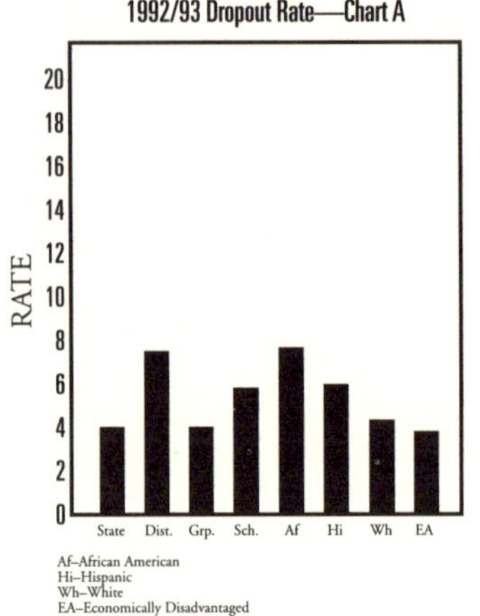

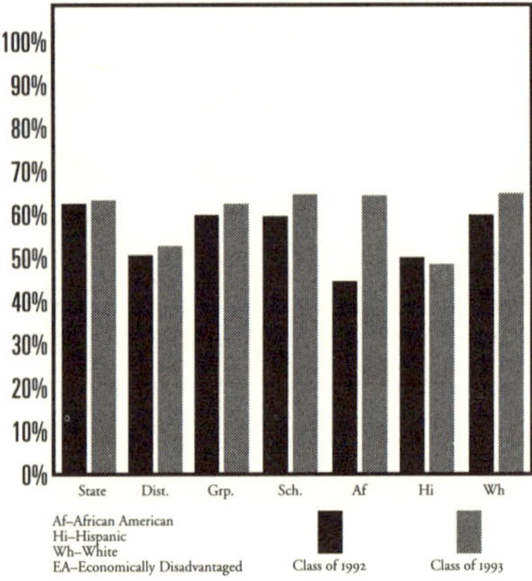

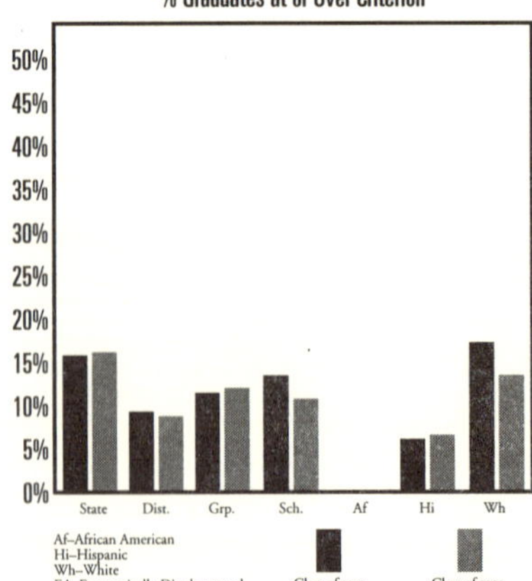

State of Texas 1994 Report Card
Sample High School
Sample ISD

Chart A shows what percent of students dropped out in the 1992-93 school year. (Shorter bars are better.) It also shows what percent of students in the state and the school district dropped out and what percent of students in the school group dropped out. The goal of the state is to reduce the drop out rate to 1% or lower

Chart B shows what percent of graduates took either the SAT (Scholastic Aptitude Test) or the ACT (American College Test). It also shows what percent of graduates in the state, district and school group took the SAT or the ACT. The goal of the state is to have at least 70% of graduates take the SAT or ACT every year.

Chart C shows what percent of graduates scored at or above the "Criterion Score" on either the SAT or ACT. The criterion score is 1000 on the SAT and 24 on the ACT. The goal of the state is to have at least 35% of graduates score above the criterion score.

The average SAT and ACT scores for the class of 1992 and 1993 are given in the table below.

	SAT		ACT	
	1992	1993	1992	1993
State	873	874	19.9	19.9
District	793	767	18.0	18.0
School	864	865	19.6	19.2
School	840	825	20.4	19.6
Af.-Am.	636	689	*	*
Hispanic	769	784	19.8	*
White	901	889	21.4	20.8

State of Texas 1994 Report Card
Sample High School
Sample ISD

School Characteristics

This section of the report card shows student and teacher characteristics for the school, the school district and the state. It also gives information on attendance, program enrollment and school finances.

Principal: Dr. Al Johnson
Total enrollment: 1,748
Grade span: 09–12

Student Characteristics

	School	District	State
% African-American	22.0	44.9	14.3
% Hispanic	21.7	38.2	34.9
% White	48.7	14.8	48.4
% Other	7.6	2.1	2.4
% Economically Disadvantaged	28.4	69.0	43.6
% Limited English Prof.	8.7	21.7	11.3
% Mobility	8.7	21.7	11.3

Teacher Characteristics

	School	District	State
% African-American	18.7	37.2	8.3
% Hispanic	12.0	8.0	13.9
% White	66.0	53.9	77.2
% Other	3.2	0.8	0.4
Students per Teacher	19.4	16.9	16.1
Average years Experience	16.6	13.7	11.3

Attendance

	School	Group	District	State
% African-Am.	88.5	88.5	88.5	88.5
% Hispanic	86.7	86.7	86.7	86.7
% White	91.7	91.7	91.7	91.7
% Other	95.0	95.0	95.0	95.0
% Total	90.2	90.2	90.2	90.2

Program Enrollment

	School	District	State
% Special Ed.	7.4	7.6	10.3
% Career and Tech.	45.0	10.8	13.6
% Bilingual/ESL	4.7	18.3	9.7
% Gifted and Talented	7.3	11.4	7.0

Financial Information

Expenditures per student

	School	District	State
Instruction	$1,919	$2,702	$2,549
Administration	$242	$257	$229
Other costs	$441	$1,171	$1,236
Total budgeted	$2,601	$4,130	$4,013

Expenditures are dollar amounts budgeted to be spent during the 1993–94 school year. Total dollar amounts have been divided by the number of students enrolled in the school. Instruction is mostly teacher salaries while administration is mostly the principal's salary. Remember that dollar amounts are per student.

School Report Card
What Does It Really Mean?

STUDENT PERFORMANCE

TAAS Test: The Texas Assessment of Academic Skills (TAAS) is a standardized test required of students in grades third, fourth, fifth, sixth, seventh, eighth, and tenth. The test measures whether a student has "mastered" the material he or she is expected to learn at that grade level. The state has set a goal that at least ninety percent of the students at a particular grade level should pass each subject area of TAAS. While this goal has yet to be reached, the state also uses other TAAS pass rates as tools to measure performance of schools. At least twenty-five percent of a school's students must pass all three sections of the test for the school to be rated as better than "low performing" by the Texas Education Agency. The agency also uses the scores to rank schools as "exemplary," "recognized," or "acceptable." A school is considered "exemplary" when ninety percent or more of its students pass all three sections of the test. "Recognized" schools must have sixty-five percent of students passing, and "acceptable" means that between twenty-five and sixty-five percent pass the three sections of the TAAS.

Based on these scores and accountability ratings, a parent can get a rough idea about how well a school is doing compared to other schools in the state.

Further, the TAAS scores can show what percentage of a school's students seem to be well prepared to move on to the next grade. It is also possible to compare students' *average* scores this year with those of last year. It is important to remember, though, that these are average scores and that until 1994 only students in grades fourth, eighth, and tenth were required to take the test. This means that comparing scores for different years can only show whether the average performance of students in a particular grade is better or worse than the year before. There is no way to tell how an individual student's performance changed, nor is there any way to be sure that the average scores include the same students for both years. Nor is it possible to compare a school's 1994 third, fifth, sixth, or seventh grade performance with that at the year before.

Finally, it is important to realize that not all students in a particular school are required to take the test and the scores of some students who do take it are not used to calculate the school averages. Special Education students and those with limited English proficiency can be exempted from the test and students who enter the school after the official census date in October are tested but not counted in the accountability measures. Still, a parent looking at TAAS scores on the various sections of the test can at least see in which areas a school's students appear to be performing well and how they compare with the other schools in the table.

Dropout Rate: The dropout rate chart reports the percentage of students in the grades offered who dropped out during the previous school year. In this chart, shorter bars or lower numbers are better. The Texas Education Agency (TEA) has set a goal of reducing the percentage of students who drop out of school to below 1 percent. The dropout rate for all schools in the 1992–93 school year was 3.8 per cent. It may be important to realize, however, that the rate is higher for certain groups and for certain schools. Schools in larger cities and those with more minority students tend to have higher dropout rates. And more students (30 percent) drop out in the ninth grade than any other. So, the various group rates presented in the chart can be more informative than simply comparing a school with the state average.

College Admission Tests: Two graphs on the report card offer information about the percentage of graduates who took either the SAT or the ACT in preparation for attending college. The Scholastic Aptitude Test (SAT) tests a student's verbal and mathematical skills. The American College Test (ACT) includes tests of reading and science reasoning in addition to English and mathematics. The state hopes to have at least seventy percent of its high school graduates take one of these tests each year and has set a goal for thirty-five percent of these students to score better than 1000 on the SAT or 24 on the ACT. These "criterion scores" have been established by the TEA as a standard of excellence.

Although the charts in the report card are helpful in comparing the percentage of graduates taking the tests and those scoring above the "criterion score" in one school with those in the district and across the state, it is important to remember that there are limitations to this comparison. There is no way, based on this information, to know how well students in a particular school compare with those in schools outside of Texas. Such information would be useful because students hoping to go to college often compete with others from other states. Even when a school does well on the report when compared with others in the district or in Texas, it is possible that it is not performing as well as, or better than, schools in other areas of the country. In fact, Texas scores on the SAT tend to be more than twenty points lower than the national average and ACT scores are also below the national average.

SCHOOL CHARACTERISTICS

Student Characteristics and Program Enrollment: While it might be interesting for a parent to know something about the other students attending a school with his or her child, the Student Characteristics section of the report card can be even more informative. Texas schools differ considerably from one area of the state to another, and these differences often have an impact on school performance. For example, schools in large cities and those with lots of minority students tend to also have more students who are economically disadvantaged. Studies have also found that where economic status is low, schools often have a larger number of students with special needs. There also tend to be more students in bilingual or English as a Second Language programs in schools in large cities and in Southwest Texas. Each of these characteristics will have an impact on the averages and percentages reported in the student performance section of the report card. So, it is important to look at this section as well when comparing an individual school with others in other parts of Texas.

Teacher Characteristics: The report card includes a table describing the teachers in the student's school as well as those at other schools in the district and the state. This information includes ethnicity and average years of experience, as well as the student/teacher ratio. The comparison of the ethnic makeup of a school's teaching staff with the student population and with the staffs of other schools is fairly straightforward. But the figure showing years of teaching experience and students per teacher may reveal more than just class size and teacher age. A school where class size (more students per teacher) is large and years of teaching experience are lower than average may be experiencing rapid growth in the numbers of students entering each year. So, while the report card only shows total enrollment for the current year, this relationship between class size and teacher experience is a way to get an idea of how that enrollment is changing over time. These characteristics are likely to have an impact on the performance scores in the other section of the report card, so it is probably a good idea to consider them together.

Financial Information: The report card sets out the number of dollars expected to be spent during the school year divided by the number of students in the school. This number becomes the "per student expenditure" and is shown for the school, its district, and for the state as a whole. There is not much information here, but what is provided may be helpful in judging school performance, or at least school management. For one thing, there is very little agreement on precisely how much money *should* be spent per student to have an effective school and of course, the total expenditures budget will depend on how much money is available in the form of tax revenue and state funds. But it can be valuable to know how the money that is spent is divided. Across the state, expenditures for instruction accounted for more than half of all school spending. If an individual school is spending less than half its funds on instruction, or is spending more than the average amount on administration or other costs, this could mean that the school is not operating as efficiently as it could or should.

CONCLUSION

The school report card is an additional tool for parents to use to judge how well their child's school is performing when compared with other schools in Texas. It is important, however, to consider the entire set of tables and charts, not just one or two. The student and teacher characteristics in the second part of the report can have an impact on the performance numbers in the first part.

Other information not given by the report card might have an impact as well. For example, the amount of tax revenue available to a school district will affect school spending; the economic status of students and their families may have an impact on performance; and a school's location and the size of its district might affect the financial, ethnic, and performance figures.

While the report card provides some statistical information about an individual school as well as an overall state average for comparison, it does not mean very much beyond that. There is little information about standards or expectations against which to measure the performance of the individual school or the entire public school system. Comparison is possible between individual schools and the state average, so it is possible to know if a particular school is performing better or worse than others. But what does that mean? For example, if the entire public school system in Texas is ranked well below those in other states, a school performing above the state average may still be doing poorly when compared to other states. Is it enough to be the best school in Texas when that means little or nothing outside the state?

Also, 1994 will be a difficult year in which to use the report card for comparison to previous years. Prior to this year, only students in the forth, eighth, and tenth grade were required to take the TAAS test. So, in some cases there are no previous scores for direct comparison. Some research also shows that students in the grades added this year tend to have higher test scores on average. This may make comparison across groups and across years more difficult to interpret as well. Finally, even without this concern, the reported scores are averages, so a parent cannot compare an individual student's performance from one year to the next, and it is highly unlikely that the average scores were achieved by the same group of students from one year to the next.

Likewise, the Accountability Rating for 1994 is not comparable to previous years. This year the Texas Education Agency changed the criteria by which schools are given this rating and by doing so moved a number of schools from Low-performing status to Acceptable, though there was little actual change in their performance. Prior to 1994, a school would be labeled Low-performing if more than twenty percent of its students failed to pass all three parts of the TAAS test. In 1993, 326 of the state's approximately 6,600 schools fell into this category. The 1994 requirements call for at least twenty-five percent of students to pass *each* of the three parts of the test. In this case different students can pass different parts, as long as twenty-five percent or more pass each part. Thus, the hurdle to overcome Low-performing status was lowered a bit— only fifty-five schools got that rating this year, while the number of Recognized schools doubled and the number of Exemplary schools tripled. The final result of these changes is that even if a school's performance rating did improve between the 1992–93 school year and 1993–94, there is no way to be sure that the actual *quality of education* improved. It is important to note, however, that statewide scores on the standardized tests have improved incrementally over the past three years. Thus, the reduction of the number of Low-performing schools and the increase in those with the higher Recognized and Exemplary ratings are not *entirely* the result of changes in the rating system.

Finally, for an individual school, a change of a few points from one year to the next is probably not very meaningful. Because the scores are averaged and do not indicate changes in performance of specific individuals, fluctuation by a point or two in either direction is neither cause for concern nor celebration. However, such changes will be important over time. A steady increase in average scores over several years would indicate a trend toward overall improvement. Such a trend, along with significant gains in areas of weakness, is something Texas parents, and the public in general, should look for and expect as efforts continue to improve the performance of the state's schools.

School Performance Management
A system for managing student academic improvement

Developed by:
Dallas Citizens Council-Chamber Education Committee
DISD Research, Planning and Evaluation Division
DISD Enhanced School-Business Partnerships

In the last few years the Dallas Citizens Council and the Greater Dallas Chamber of Commerce have collaborated to find new ways for business to be more effective in supporting programs of the Dallas Independent School District (DISD). This effort led to the development of a program called Enhanced School Business Partnerships. These partnerships are part of the Chamber's Partners in Education program supporting the DISD. The Enhanced Partnerships focus on the use of analytical tools to facilitate the identification of specific needs. Once the needs have been identified, programs can be planned and implemented to help improve student academic performance.

Most schools go through a process of analyzing data on school performance, preparing a School Improvement Plan (SIP), and then implementing their plan.

Because a normal part of business activity is the development of useful information from a variety of data, the business partners can help schools in the analytical process. The analytical skills of the business partner can address the extensive data provided the schools to produce useful information for the principal. From this information the principal and the business partner, together, can decide where to focus available support that will most improve student student performance.

The Research, Planning and Evaluation Division of the DISD provides the schools excellent data on their school performance. This data can then be reduced to various formats desired by the principal and teachers. Reducing this data is where the business partner can be of assistance.

Several procedures have been developed that will display the data in a way most useful to a principal. By collecting these various ideas, together with suggestions and cooperation from the Research, Planning and Evaluation Division, a process has emerged that seems to have application to most schools. This process consists of four levels.

- Level 1   School rank within DISD "Effective School" Ranking.
- Level 2   Subject (and Attendance)-by-grade rank within school vs. other schools.
- Level 3   Class-by-subject change in Grade Equivalent rank within grade.
- Level 4   Student Performance change in Grade Equivalent within class.

In addition a form to set school performance goals (by grade, by subject) based on past performance is provided.

Note: This report reviews the School Performance Management Program including the tables and graphs used in analyzing available data as a basis for developing improvement plans and action programs. The detailed procedure for producing the tables and charts are not included and will be described in a separate paper.

Level 1

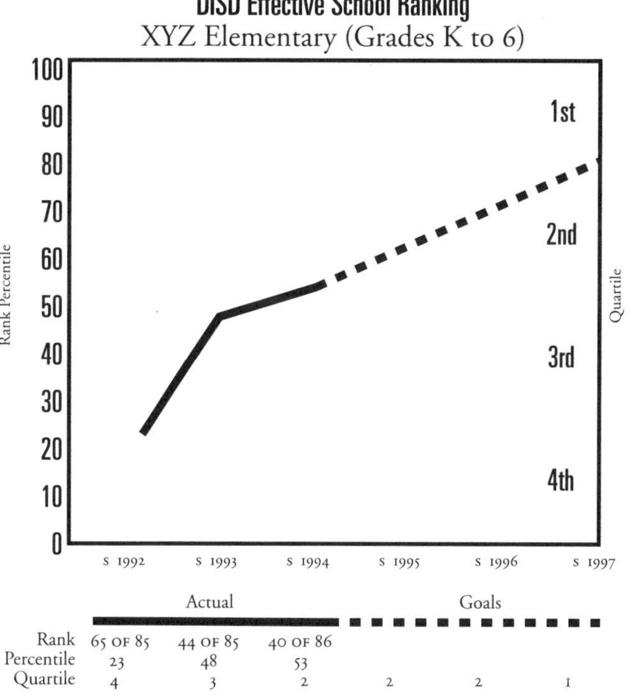

Rank	65 OF 85	44 OF 85	40 OF 86			
Percentile	23	48	53			
Quartile	4	3	2	2	2	1

LEVEL 1

Description:

The Level 1 graph shows the percentile ranks and the quartile levels for total school performance as measured by the DISD Effectiveness School Ranking System.

Purpose:

This graph shows the ranking trends for the total school and provides a framework for establishing future performance goals.

Example:

To illustrate the use of the Level 1 graph, results for a hypothetical K-6 school are shown. Using the DISD Effective School Ranking System, the XYZ Elementary School had a fourth quartile performance in the 1991–92 school year and were ranked sixty-five out of eighty-five K-6 schools or at the twenty-third percentile. The following year the performance rank improved to the forty-eighth percentile. For the 1993–94 school year the school's performance moved into the second quartile and the school leaders have set a goal to improve their school's total performance to first quartile level by the 1996–97 school year.

Level 2

DISD Effective School Ranking
XYZ Elementary (Grades K to 6)
Spring 1994

Item	Grade	Ranking Weight	1994 Rank Percentile	1993–94* Percentile Points Gain/Loss
TAAS–M	4	4	82	
TAAS–SS	4	1	78	
Math	6	2	73	-8
TAAS–R	5	5	68	
Attendance	5	1	63	4
Reading	5	2	61	24
TAAS–M	6	4	60	
Math	4	2	59	18
TAAS–M	3	4	57	
Math	5	2	56	-3
TAAS–R	6	5	56	
Math	1	2	54	8
TAAS–R	4	5	52	
TAAS–M	5	4	51	
TAAS–W	4	1	49	
Reading	4	2	48	15
Attendance	3	1	46	11
TAAS–R	3	5	45	
Attendance	2	1	42	-22
Reading	6	2	40	26
Attendance	6	1	39	-15
Reading	1	2	37	5
Attendance	4	1	35	-18
Reading	3	2	31	-7
Math	2	2	27	8
TAAS–Sci	4	1	24	
Math	3	2	24	-12
Reading	2	2	20	6
Attendance	1	1	17	-22

*TAAS not considered in 1993 ranking

LEVEL 2
Description:

The Level 2 table shows the rank percentiles and the ranking weights used in the DISD Effective School Ranking System in the Spring of 1994 for many of the various items used to evaluate school performance for the 1993–94 school year.

Purpose:

This Level 2 table provides a convenient summary for the Principal and Business Partner to use in profiling the strength and weaknesses within the overall school performance. This table can help determine the areas of greatest need and the activities which can benefit the most by focusing available resources from the school and the business partner.

Example:

Again, the hypothetical XYZ Elementary School (grades K–6) is used to illustrate the potential use of this table. A line has been drawn at the fiftieth rank percentile level. All subjects and activities above this line rank in the upper one-half of all other similar activities within the school district and all ranked below the line are in the lower one-half.

For this hypothetical case the following observations can be made:
- Five of the six grade-attendance records are in the lower one-half.
- Five of the six grade-reading results are in the lower one-half.

Principals and teachers must work to improve performance in all areas, but this ranking suggests that the school could benefit from an Attendance Improvement Program and a Reading Improvement Program with focused support from the Business Partner.

LEVEL 3 AND 4
Description:

The data for Levels 1 and 2 discussed on previous pages are from the relative ranking information in the Effectiveness Ranking System. The data for Levels 3 and 4 to be discussed next are from individual student grades on the standardized tests which are reported by Grade-Equivalents. (These results are from the ITBS-type tests and do not include the pass-fail TAAS test results.)

The individual student information for this Input Data Table is confidential and must be protected. One approach is for the school to supply the test results using sequence numbers instead of student names or identification numbers. The analytical work and displays for Levels 3and 4 can be done with sequence numbers and later the school can relate the students' name with the appropriate sequence number.

Information is required from two consecutive years of test results. This allows year-to-year delta gains to be calculated as well as providing absolute test results in grade-equivalent levels. In this case test scores from the Spring of 1994 and the Spring of 1993 provide the input data.

Purpose:

This data table provides the inputs required for the Level 3 and 4 analysis discussed on the following pages.

Levels 3 and 4

Input Data Table

School ________ Teacher ________ Class ________	1993 Reading Total	1994 Reading Total	Difference +/-	1993 Language Total	1994 Language Total	Difference +/-	1993 Math Total	1994 Math Total	Difference +/-	1993 Core Total	1994 Core Total	Difference +/-
Student's Name												

LEVEL 3
Description:

The Level 3 table shows the performance ranking in a specific subject area for the different classes within a grade at a given school. In this table the classes in a second grade are ranked by their gains from the previous year.

Purpose:

This analysis helps identify the classes within a grade with below average gains from the previous year test scores. This approach can guide additional studies in areas of weak performance.

Example:

In the Level 2 table for the XYZ Elementary School (K–6 second-grade reading was at the twentieth percentile rank and was next to the lowest item ranked for the entire school. This Level 3 breakout shows that the average gain in second-grade reading was a 0.7 delta Grade-Equivalent (GE) or six months of gain for nine months of school.

In this example there are five second-grade classes with gains ranging from 1.4 △ GEs to 0.2 △ GEs or stated another way from thirteen △ mos. gain in nine months school to only two △ mos. gain in nine months school. The lowest performing classes are clearly areas needing improvement.

LEVEL 3

School Class Ranking
XYZ Elementary (Grades K to 6)

Second-Grade Reading						
Spring 1994						
Rank	Class	Teacher	S'93 GE	S '94 GE	△ GE	△ Mos/9 Mos School
1	2C		1.6	3.0	1.4	13
2	2B		1.5	2.3	0.8	7
3	2D		1.8	2.5	0.7	6
4	2E		1.6	2.0	0.4	4
5	2A		1.7	1.9	0.2	2
				Grade Averages	0.7	6

Level 4
Description:

The Level 4 chart shows the performance on a given subject by individual students within specific classes. The small table in the upper right hand corner summarizes the overall class performance using class medians. The chart lists for each student the previous years Grade-Equivalent (GE) score, the current years score and the year-to-year △ GE. The bars show the s GE values graphically. The students are ranked by the previous year GEs with the lowest score at the bottom and the highest at the top and are compared to the Class and the U.S. Medians.

Purpose:

This chart shows how the performance of individual students relate to total class performance. Many different patterns emerge. In some classes all students make significant gains. In other classes all students have poor gains. In some classes, high performing students make strong additional gains and low performing students make modest gains. In other classes the reverse is true. Many times in a class with overall strong gains individual students will have lower GE scores than the previous year suggesting the possible need for special attention.

Example:

These Level 4 charts display student reading test scores for two second-grade classes from the hypothetical XYZ Elementary School. These classes, 2C and 2A, are top ranked and lowest ranked classes from the Level 3 table.

The top ranked 2C class shown at the top has fifteen students with scores from the previous year. This student group had a median GE score if 1.6 the previous year in first-grade tests, or 0.2 GEs below the U.S. median. The median score in the current year for the second-grade was a GE of 3.0—a delta gain of 1.4 GEs and 0.2 GEs above the U.S. median. There are significant gains for all students with one exception suggesting the need for possible special individual attention.

The lowest ranked class, 2A, has only 17 students. This group had a median GE score of 1.7 in their first-grade tests, only 0.1 GE below the U.S. median. However, the median GE score from the current year second-grade tests was only 1.9—a delta gain of only 0.2 GEs leaving the median reading level for this group of second-grade students 1.9 GEs or almost a full year below the U.S. median. All of the students had either modest gains or lower scores than the previous year. In fact, seven out of seventeen students had negative deltas from the previous year. This class is clearly in need of improvement programs.

Level 4

School Performance Analysis
1993–94 School Year

School: XYZ Elementary
1994 Grade: 2
Class: 2c
Subject: Reading

Summary:	Number of Students:	15
	S '94 Median GE:	3.0
	S '93 Median GE:	1.6
	S '93 to S '94 Grade Equivalent Gain:	1.4
	S '93 to S '94 Months Gain/9 Mo. School:	12.6

△ Grade Equivalent

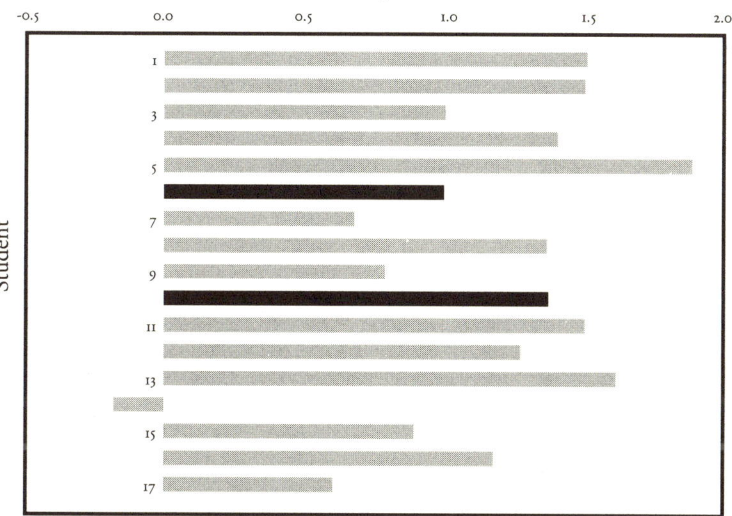

No.	Student Seq. No.	Name	Grade Equivalent S 1993	S 1994	△ +/-
1	1		3.0	4.5	1.5
2	2		2.2	3.7	1.5
3	3		2.1	3.1	1.0
4	4		1.9	3.3	1.4
5	5		1.8	3.7	1.9
6	**U.S. Median**		**1.8**	**2.8**	**1.0**
7	6		1.7	2.4	0.7
8	7		1.7	3.1	1.4
9	8		1.6	2.4	0.8
10	**Class Median**		**1.6**	**3.0**	**1.4**
11	9		1.5	3.0	1.5
12	10		1.4	2.7	1.3
13	11		1.4	3.0	1.6
14	12		1.3	1.1	-0.2
15	13		1.1	2.0	0.9
16	14		1.1	2.3	1.2
17	15		1.0	1.6	0.6

School Performance Analysis (Continued)

School: XYZ Elementary
1994 Grade: 2
Class: 2c
Subject: Reading

Summary:	Number of Students:	17
	S '94 Median GE:	1.9
	S '93 Median GE:	1.7
S '93 to S '94 Grade Equivalent Gain:		0.2
S '93 to S '94 Months Gain/9 Mo. School:		1.8

△ Grade Equivalent

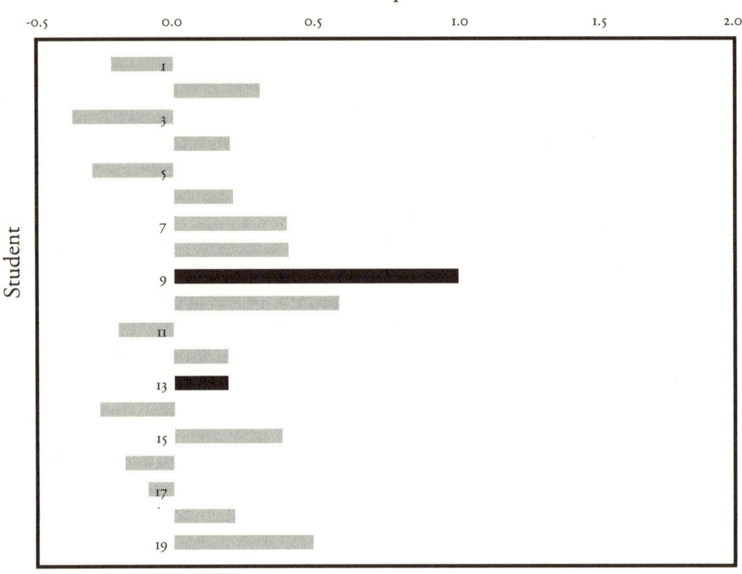

No.	Student Seq. No.	Name	Grade Equivalent S 1993	S 1994	△ +/-
1	1		3.0	2.8	-0.2
2	2		2.5	2.8	0.3
3	3		2.4	2.0	-0.4
4	4		2.4	2.6	0.2
5	5		2.2	1.9	-0.3
6	6		2.0	2.2	0.2
7	7		1.9	2.3	0.4
8	8		1.8	2.2	0.4
9	**U.S. Median**		**1.8**	**2.8**	**1.0**
10	9		1.7	2.3	0.6
11	10		1.7	1.5	-0.2
12	11		1.7	1.9	0.2
13	**Class Median**		**1.7**	**1.9**	**0.2**
14	12		1.6	1.3	-0.3
15	13		1.5	1.9	0.4
16	14		1.5	1.3	-0.2
17	15		1.3	1.2	-0.1
18	16		1.3	1.5	0.2
19	17		1.2	1.7	0.5

School Performance Planning Matrix Form

Description:

This form is designed to help schools develop reasonable three-year goals based on the most recent performance levels and trends within their school. For a given subject area, such as reading, it shows the Grade-Equivalent (GE) scores and year-to-year $\triangle$ GEs for all of the grades in the school and provides spaces for developing future goals by year and grade.

Purpose:

This matrix form provides a high level summary planning tool for the principal and all teachers involved in providing instruction in a given subject area. The final result—sixth-grade reading capability—is a function of the student gains year-by-year from kindergarten through the sixth grade. If students are to leave sixth-grade with median reading skills at the U.S. median level 6.8 GEs or better, the $\triangle$ GE gains each year must average 1.0 GEs or better. If the starting kindergarten GE is below the U.S. median of 0.8 or if a class falls below a 1.0 $\triangle$ GE gain in a given year then there must be above average gains in other grades in later years to make up the short-fall.

This matrix chart shows recent trends and goals for each grade and shows how the individual year-by-year gains relate to the total school goal for six-grade reading capability.

Example:

In this example for the hypothetical XYZ Elementary School, the median GE for sixth-grade reading in the Spring of 1994 was 5.8, or one full year below the U.S. median. The principal and teachers have set goals for the next three years which will result in higher reading scores in every grade, a sixth-grade GE score at the 6.8 GE U.S. median level, and an on-going capability at every grade which will result in future sixth-grade classes performing above the U.S. median.

As shown in the Level 2 Ranking List, second-grade reading ranked the lowest. In this matrix the second-grade 0.7 $\triangle$ GE for the 1993–94 school year was the lowest of all the grades. The Level 3 table shows how the second-grade classes rank with Class 2A at the bottom of the performance rank with a $\triangle$ GE gain of only 0.2 GEs. The Level 4 charts show how the individual students in Class 2A scored in comparison to the above average capability gains made in Class 2C.

These analytical methods can be used as appropriate for all subjects, grades, and classes to provide guidance for developing Improvement Plans and Action Programs, including selected target programs for focusing the business partner support.

Planning Matrix Form

School Performance Actuals/Goals
XYZ Elementary (K–6)

Reading

School Year → Grade ↓	Actuals				Goals	
	1991–92	1992–93	1993–94	1994–95	1995–96	1996–97
K GE (Core)	0.4	0.5	0.5	0.6	0.7	0.8
1st GE △ GE	1.6	1.5 1.1	1.4 0.9	1.5 1.0	1.7 1.1	1.8 1.1
2nd GE △ GE	2.0	2.3 0.7	2.2 0.7	2.2 0.8	2.5 1.0	2.7 1.0
3rd GE △ GE	2.8	2.9 0.9	3.2 0.9	3.2 1.0	3.3 1.1	3.6 1.1
4th GE △ GE	3.8	4.0 1.2	4.0 1.1	4.4 1.2	4.4 1.2	4.5 1.2
5th GE △ GE	5.1	5.0 1.2	5.1 1.1	5.1 1.1	5.6 1.2	5.6 1.2
6th GE △ GE	5.9	6.0 0.9	5.8 0.8	6.1 1.0	6.2 1.1	6.8 1.2

PERFORMANCE ANALYSIS RESPONSE

Once a School Performance Analysis has been made, there are several ways to respond. The most important is to adjust the School Improvement Plan (SIP) to include the needs identified. The principal may review the analysis with the school faculty, the school SCE Council and the Area Director for additional inputs. Based on the analysis and inputs from others, the decision on specific "action" programs can be made. In some cases the action will be an intervention program (e.g., a tutor program for certain grades). In other cases the action will be a parent or community program(e.g., an attendance improvement program). There may be teachers who need specific instructional or subject matter training. There may be organizational needs where the whole school takes specific training (e.g., Total Quality Management, TQM).

Regardless of the response to the analysis, the business partner can work with the principal to secure the required resources. This action closes the loop on the performance analysis. However, an analysis should be performed each year so as to determine if the corrective actions were effective and to identify new needs.

Charter schools:
Eleven states have them; more on the way

State	Year passed	Schools allowed	Active schools	Autonomy*	Details
Arizona	1994	Unlimited	None	More	Only state to include a $1 million, start-up fund enabling charter schools to receive grants up to $100,000 for each of two years. An unlimited number can be sponsored by local boards; 25 a year per state board.
California	1992	100 maximum	63	More	Groups, individuals and entire districts can apply for charter status. Sponsors include local school boards or county boards of education.
Colorado	1993	50 before 1997; then unlimited	14	More	13 schools are set aside for at risk students. Group or individuals, with the support of parents, can obtain a charter from a local school board. The state board has the power to overturn a local board's rejection.
Georgia	1993	Unlimited	None	Less	Only the faculty or staff of a school, with the support of parents and the local school board, can organize a charter. Only existing public schools can be converted.
Hawaii	1994	No more than 25	None	Less	The schools must be organized by a local school board, which must obtain the support of three-fifths of the school's administration, faculty and parents.
Kansas	1994	15 schools statewide (two per district)	None	Less	Charters must be approved by a local school board and the state

State	Year passed	Schools allowed	Active schools	Autonomy*	Details
Mass.	1993	25	15	More	Considered one of the most liberal laws. Schools can be organized by two or more certified teachers, 10 or more parents or any other person or group granted a charter by the state secretary of education. Won't begin until the 1995-96 school year.
Michigan	1993	Unlimited	7	More	Called "public school academies." Organizers can be any individual or group. Charters can be granted by local or regional school district, community colleges and state public universities.
Minn.	1991	35	13	More	The first state to pass a charter law.
New Mex.	1993	5	None	Less	Will remain under the legal authority of school districts. Some administrative costs may be withheld by school districts.
Wisconsin	1993	20	None	Less	Required the state superintendent of education to approve the first 10 requests received. Local school boards or an individual with the support of a certain percentage of teachers can organize charter schools. A school board can convert all of its schools to charter status if 50 percent of the teachers in the district sign the petition and if arrangements are made for students who don't want to attend a charter school. Schools remain under local district control.

* Experts have divided state laws into two group; those that allow schools more autonomy and those that allow less. Those with more autonomy are generally free from the authority of the local school board. Such schools act as nonprofit corporations. Those with less autonomy remain under the authority of their local board, and are not automatically exempt from most state laws and district policy.

SOURCE: The Morrison Institute for Public Policy at Arizona State University School of Public Affairs and Fort Worth Star Telegram

Agency/Programs to be Eliminated, Transferred or Combined
Agency/Program

1. Commission on the Arts
2. Department on Aging*
3. Aircraft Pooling Board Brucellosis Program
4. Department of Aviation
5. Board of Barber Examiners
6. Department of Community Affairs
7. Department of Commerce*
8. Cosmetology Commission
9. Office of Consumer Protection
10. Finance Commission
11. Fire Department Emergency Board
12. Commission on Fire Protection Personnel Standard and Education
13. Board of Examiners in the Fitting and Dispensing of Hearing Aids
14. Board of Irrigators
15. Law Enforcement Management Institute
16. Department of Licensing and Regulation
17. Council on Offenders with Mental Impairments
18. Motor Vehicle Commission Local Parks Fund Coastal Beach Services
19. Board of Plumbing Examiners
20. Board of Polygraph Examiners
21. State Securities Board
22. Soil and Water Conservation Board
23. Interagency Council on Sex Offender Treatment
24. Public Utility Commission
25. Office of Public Utility Counsel
26. Veteran's Commission
27. Water Well Drillers Board Public Interest Advocate
28. Canadian River Compact Commissioner
29. Pecos River Compact Commissioner
30. Red River Compact Commissioner
31. Rio Grande River Compact Commissioner
32. Sabine River Compact Commissioner
33. Cancer Council Children's Outreach Heart Program Hope Center for Youth
34. Health and Human Services Coordinating Council Baylor College of Dentistry
35. Texas Agricultural Extension Service
36. Animal Damage Control Service
37. Texas Food and Fibers Commission

Study Rules

The following are suggested study rules; however, it would be appropriate for the parent and student to prepare the rules together.

1. Ask the child how his/her day was and if he has homework. This lets him open up to talk about bad days, good days, or school gossip.

2. Allow your child to relax for one hour with a good snack—fruit, popcorn, or juice (no candy or soft drinks). Allow your child to watch TV, jump, run, bike ride, or talk on the phone before homework.

3. After the hour break, talk about the homework. Find out what has to be done and if your child needs some help. Divide the subjects up between parents.

4. Set the location — homework can be done at the kitchen table — but no TV, radio, or other small children. If necessary have the other parent take care of the small children in another area during this time. Homework is brought home to help and aid in understanding assignments but let your child know that the homework will not be done for him.

5. When studying the night before a test, drill the questions with your child until he feels confident with the correct answers (no matter how long it takes). Make it fun; help your child pick out key words in questions to help him associate with the answers. Get up 30 minutes earlier in the morning to review again.

6. If your child comes home from school needing something for the next dayís assignment (book, picture, article) help him get it.

7. Do not let other children in the house bother the child and parent who are working on homework.

8. Do not allow phone calls during homework or after bedtime.

9. Some children who do not do well on tests are afraid to tell their parents. Explain to the child that if he/she does not talk to you about it then you will be unable to help him/her. Do not ground, spank, or scream.

10. Make sure he/she has a good snack, well-balanced meals, clean clothes, and is in bed on time. Let the child read a book or watch TV until it is time for bed. Donít rough house before bedtime.

11. Let the child have one extra curricular activity during school.

12. Do not make too many demands on the child during school. Have the child make his/her bed, keep the bathroom straight, and feed the pet. During the school week, school, peers, and homework is enough.

Source: TEPSA, Spring 1987

What Should Parents Expect
From Their Child's School?
A Checklist for Concerned Parents

What are my child's standardized test scores?

These can be statewide or nationwide tests. Some tests show percentile scores-if your child has a high percentile, say 80th percent, then he or she is performing well. A low percentile, say 25th percent, means probably the child has a significant weakness in that area. You will need to work with the school to find out exactly what can be done to correct that weakness. Statewide Texas Assessment of Academic Skills (TAAS) test scores are either "pass" or "fail"—if your child fails a portion of the TAAS in high school, he or she cannot graduate until that portion is passed.

How do I compare my child's grades with standardized test scores?

Sometimes children receive A's and B's on the report card, but standardized tests may show that the child's skills really are not that strong. Watch out for "grade inflation" - where report card grades do not show the child's actual skill levels. Children who perform poorly on standardized tests, yet have fairly good grades, should be evaluated by the school on individual achievement tests to determine actual skill levels.

How much homework should my child bring home?

Your child should have homework every night and you should hear from the school if your child is not doing his or her homework. If your child is forgetting or not doing the homework, the teacher should be willing to set up a daily or weekly communication system with you so you can monitor exactly what your child should be doing.

What other things should I look for to see how well my child is doing in school?

You should receive a regular folder or stapled stack of graded papers along with information on classroom behavior and upcoming school events and activities. Go over these papers one by one with your child. A child's graded papers should have specific comments as to why an item is incorrect or how the work could be improved. If behavioral problems exist, are there clear examples of incidents that have occurred? A weekly folder should include teacher comments and require your signature and comments.

How do I know if my child's school is responding well to the public it serves?

Request to receive standardized test scores for the entire school. Compare these scores to national averages. Additionally, schedule visits with the school's principal and teachers. When you ask to meet with school personnel or send a note or question, your request should be honored quickly and efficiently. You should sense a friendly atmosphere where the entire staff seems to like, care about and interact well with students. Volunteers should be welcomed and utilized efficiently.

Does my child's school have a strong curriculum in the basic skills?

This is probably the most important factor in a student's education, yet one most parents lack the confidence to question. Make sure that your child is receiving instruction in all basic skills, Ask to see exactly how reading, math, grammar, spelling, composition, geography, etc. are being taught. You should see clear evidence that these skills are being systematically and rigorously taught.

Composition instruction should include using spelling and grammar. Instruction in how to read words one does not know should be available to any child who is having difficulty.

How well should my child be able to read from his or her textbooks?

If your child has continued difficulty reading aloud in a fluent manner from his or her texts, the child will also have trouble understanding schoolwork in general. Make sure the school is offering specific help in learning *how* to read if this is the case.

High school students should be learning vocabulary lists and should be reading books on a regular basis.

Ask questions to determine if your child is receiving a rigorous curriculum.

Is my child expected to produce, on a regular basis, a *well* done final work product?

Should parents expect daily assignments to be completed neatly and correctly? On significant written assignments, you should expect well-done cursive writing, complete sentences, correct spelling and grammar, clean paper, etc. Classroom assignments should show a balance of group projects, activity-oriented learning, and significant, well-executed written assignments.

No question is silly or stupid. If you do not understand something, keep asking questions until you are sure you do understand.

Adapted from a pamphlet by Public Education Network

SELECTED BIBLIOGRAPHY

Aldridge, John S., Susan F. Heiligenthal, and Chris G. Elizalde. 1982. *Handbook for Texas School District Governance.* Austin, TX: Texas Association of School Boards.

American Legislative Exchange Council. 1994. *Report Card On American Education 1994: A State by State Analysis.* Washington, DC: American Legislative Exchange Council. September 9.

Bennett, William J. 1994. *The Index of Leading Cultural Indicators: Facts and Figures on the State of American Society.* New York: Simon and Schuster.

Bennett, William J. 1988. *American Education: Making It Work.* Washington, DC: United States Department of Education.

Bissenger, H. G. 1990. *Friday Night Lights: a Town, a Team, and a Dream.* Reading, MA: Addison-Wesley Publishing Company.

Bowser, Jack E. 1989. *Educating America: Lessons Learned in the Nation's Corporations.* New York: John Wiley and Sons, Inc.

Boyer, Ernest L. 1991. *Ready to Learn: A Mandate for the Nation.* Princeton, NJ: The Carnegie Foundation for the Advancement of Teaching.

Boyer, Ernest L. 1983. *High School, A Report on Secondary Education in America.* New York: Harper and Row.

Brooks, A. Phillips. 1994. "TEA Says Schools Are Improving But 'A Long Journey' Remains Ahead." *The Dallas Morning News.* August 3.

Bryce, Robert. 1992. "Prison Facts." *The Austin Chronicle.* September 25. p. 36.

Bunzel, John H., ed. 1985. *Challenge to American Schools: The Case for Standards and Values.* New York: Oxford University Press.

Center For Texas Studies, National Center for Policy Analysis. 1990. *Equality and Inequality in Texas School Finance.* Dallas: Center For Texas Studies.

Cetron, Marvin and Margaret Gayle. 1991. *Educational Renaissance; Our Schools at the Turn of the Century.* New York: St. Martin's Press.

Chira, Susan. 1993. "Is Smaller Better? Educators Now Say Yes For High School." *New York Times,* July 14. p. A1.

Chubb, John E. and Terry M. Moe. 1990. *Politics, Markets, Markets, and America's Schools.* Washington, D.C.: The Brookings Institution.

Cohen, Michael. 1988. *Restructuring the Education System: Agenda for the 1990s.* Washington, DC: National Governors' Association.

Coles, Gerald. 1987. *The Learning Mystique: A Critical Look at "Learning Disabilities."* New York: Pantheon Books.

D.C. Committee on Public Education. 1989. *Our Children, Our Future: Revitalizing the District of Columbia Public Schools.* The D.C. Committee on Public Education.

D.C. Committee on Public Education. 1989. *Our Children, Our Future: Revitalizing the District of Columbia Public Schools; Executive Summary.* The D.C. Committee on Public Education.

David, Jane L., Michael Cohen, Dean Honetschlager, and Susan Traiman. 1990. *State Actions to Restructure Schools: First Steps.* Washington, DC: National Governor's Association.

David, Jane L. 1989. *Restructuring in Progress: Lessons From Pioneering Districts.* Washington, DC: National Governor's Association.

Davidson, Dr. Jack L. 1983. *An Analysis of Reports on the Status of Education in America: Findings, Recommendations, and Implications.* Tyler, TX: Tyler Independent School District.

Drucker, Peter F. 1994. "The Age of Social Transformation." *The Atlantic Monthly.* 247:3 November. pp. 53–80.

Elmore, Richard F., and Associates. 1990. *Restructuring Schools: the Next Generation of Education Reform.* San Francisco: Josey Bass.

Elmore, Richard F. 1988. *Early Experience in Restructuring Schools: Voices from the Field.* Washington, DC: National Governor's Association.

Ferguson, Ronald F. 1991. "Paying for Education: New Evidence on How and Why Money Matters." *Harvard Journal on Legislation.* Vol. #28: 465–498.

Finn, Chester E., Jr. 1992. *Education Reform in the '90s.* New York: MacMillan.

Finn, Chester E., Jr. 1991. *We Must Take Charge: Our Schools and Our Future.* New York: The Free Press.

Fiske, Edward B. 1991. *Smart Schools, Smart Kids: Why Do Some School Work?* New York: Simon and Schuster.

Frady, Marshall. 1992. "Profiles: Outsider." *The New Yorker*, 67:52. February 17, pp. 39–69.

Gerstner, Louis V. 1994. *Reinventing Education: Entrepreneurship in America's Public Schools.* New York: Dutton.

Gimlin, Hoyt, and Martha V. Gottron, eds. 1985. *Education Report Card: Schools on the Line.* Washington: Congressional Quarterly, Inc.

Goodland, John I. 1994. *Education Renewal: Better Teachers, Better Schools.* San Francisco: Josey Bass.

Goodland, John I. 1990. *Teachers For Our Nation's Schools.* San Francisco: Josey Bass.

Goodwin, Doris Kearns. 1994. *No Ordinary Time: Franklin and Eleanor Roosevelt; The Home Front in World War II.* New York: Simon and Schuster.

Guthrie, James. 1989. "Why Principals Should First Be Teachers." *Education Digest,* (March) V54:7 pp. 13-16.

Hamberg, David A. 1992. *Today's Children: Creating a Future for a Generation in Crisis.* New York: Times Books.

Hammond, Linda Darling, and Barnett Berry. 1988. *The Evolution of a Teacher Policy.* Washington, DC: Center for Policy Research in Education.

Hancock, Lynell. 1994. "In Defiance of Darwin: How a Public School in The Bronx Turns Dropouts into Scholars." *Newsweek.* October 24, p. 61.

Hanusheck, Eric. 1994. *Making Schools Work: Improving Performance and Controlling Costs.* Washington, D. C.: The Brookings Institution.

Hill, Paul T., Arthur E. Wise, and Leslie Shapiro. 1989. *Educational Progress: Cities Mobilize to Improve Their Schools.* Santa Monica, CA: The Rand Corporation.

Hirsch, E.D., Jr. 1987. *Cultural Literacy: What Every American Needs to Know.* Boston: Houghton Mifflin Company.

Hoffman, James V. and Sara A. Edwards, eds. 1986. *Reality and Reform In Clinical teacher Education.* New York: Random House.

Holmes Group, The. 1990. Tomorrow's Schools: *Principle for the Design of Professional Development Schools.* East Lansing, MI: The Holmes Group.

Johnson, Susan Moore. 1990. *Teachers at Work: Achieving Success in Our Schools.* New York: Basic Books, Inc.

Kagan, Sharon L., and Edward F. Zigler. 1987. *Early Schooling: The National Debate.* New Haven: Yale University Press.

Kearns, David T., and Denise P. Doyle. 1989. *Winning the Brain Race: A Bold Plan to Make Our Schools Competitive.* San Francisco: Institute for Contemporary Studies.

Kemerer, Frank R., and Jim Walsh. 1994. *The Educator's Guide to Texas School Law.* Austin: University of Texas Press.

Kidder, Tracy. 1989. *Among Schoolchildren.* Boston: Houghton Mifflin.

Kirst, Michael W. 1984. *Who Controls Our Schools? American Values in Conflict.* New York: W. H. Freeman and Company.

Kozol, Jonathan. 1991. *Savage Inequalities: Children in America's Schools*. New York: Crown Publishers, Inc.

Kunde, Diana. 1994. "Higher Education Does Pay, Says Census Bureau Figures." *The Dallas Morning News*. July 22. p. D1.

League of Women Voters Education Fund. 1993. *Juvenile Violence and the Juvenile Justice System in Texas*. Austin, TX: League of Women Voters.

Levine, Marsha. *School Reform: A Role for the American Business Community*.

Lightfoot, Sara Lawrence. 1983. *The Good High School: Portraits of Character and Culture*. New York: Basic Books, Inc.

Lieberman, Myron. 1993. *Public Education: An Autopsy*. Cambridge, Mass: Harvard University Press.

Lyndon B. Johnson School of Public Affairs. 1993. *A Decade of Change: Public Education Reform in Texas, 1981-1992: Special Project Report*. Austin: Lyndon B. Johnson School of Public Affairs and Texas Education Agency.

Lyndon B. Johnson School of Public Affairs. 1988. *Education, Technology, and the Texas Economy, Volume 1: Economics of Education*. Austin: Lyndon B. Johnson School of Public Affairs and Texas Education Agency.

Lyndon B. Johnson School of Public Affairs. 1989. *Education, Technology, and the Texas Economy, Volume 2: Can Technology Help Texas Public Schools?*. Austin: Lyndon B. Johnson School of Public Affairs and Texas Education Agency.

Lyndon B. Johnson School of Public Affairs. 1989. *Education, Technology, and the Texas Economy, Volume 3: Vocational Preparation.* Austin: Lyndon B. Johnson School of Public Affairs and Texas Education Agency.

Maeroff, Gene I. 1982. *Don't Blame the Kids; The Trouble With America's Public Schools.* New York: McGraw Hill.

Manno, Bruno V. 1994. "Outcome Based Education: Miracle Cure or Plague?" Hudson Briefing Paper: Shaping the Future. 165 (June). The Hudson Institute.

Marshall, Ray and Marc Tucker. 1992. *Thinking for a Living: Education and the Wealth of Nations.* New York: Basic Books.

Murphy, John and Jeffry Schiller. 1992. *Transforming America's Schools: Administrators' Call To Action.* La Salle, Illinois: Open Court.

National Center For Education Statistics. 1994. *The Nation's Report Card.* Washington, D.C.: Office of Educational Research and Improvement, U. S. Department of Education.

National Center For Education Statistics. 1989. *Education Indicators.* Washington, DC: U. S. Department of Education.

National Commission on Children. 1991. *Beyond Rhetoric: A New American Agenda for Children and Families: Final Report.* Washington, D.C. The National Commission on Children.

National Commission on Excellence in Education. 1983. *A Nation at Risk: The Imperative for Educational Reform.* Washington, DC: National Commission on Excellence in Education.

National Education Goals Panel. 1994. *The National Education Goals Report.* Washington, D.C.

National Governors' Association. 1990. *Educating America: State Strategies for Achieving the National Education Goals: Report of the Task Force on Education.* Washington, DC: National Governors' Association.

National Issues Forum. 1983. *Priorities for the Nation's Schools.* Dayton, Ohio: Domestic Policy Association.

National Research Council. 1989. *Everybody Counts: A Report to the Nation on the Future of Mathematics Education.* Washington, DC: National Academy Press.

Papert, Seymour. 1993. *The Children's Machine: Rethinking School in the Age of the Computer.* New York: Basic Books, Inc.

Peterson, Paul E. 1983. *Making the Grade: Report of the Twentieth Century Fund Task Force on Federal Elementary and Secondary Education Policy.* New York: The Twentieth Century Fund.

Probe Commission. 1993. *Imagine…Providence Blueprint for Education.* Providence, RI: Public Education Fund.

Ravitch, Diane, and Chester E. Finn, Jr. 1987. *What Do Our 17-Year-Olds Know? A Report on the First National Assessment of History and Literature.* New York: Harper and Row.

Ravitch, Diane. 1983. *The Troubled Crusade: American Education 1945-1980.* New York: Basic Books.

Schneider, Barbara and James S. Coleman, eds. 1993. *Parents, Their Children, and Schools.* Boulder, CO: Westview Press.

Select Committee on Public Education. July, 1984. *Review of Teacher Perceptions of Paperwork Requirements.* Austin.

Select Committee on Public Education. April 19, 1984. Recommendations. Austin.

Sewall, Gilbert C. 1983. *Necessary Lessons: Decline and Renewal in American Schools.* New York: The Free Press.

Shanker, Albert. 1988. *"State of Our Union" Address Before the American Federation of Teachers.* San Francisco, California. July 2.

Shanker, Albert. 1988. "Public Relations or Public Disclosure: School Failure Needs Airing." New York Times September 11.

Sharp, John. 1994. *Forces of Change: Shaping the Future of Texas.* Austin: Office of The Texas Comptroller of Public Accounts.

Sharp, John R. 1993. *Texas Education Agency: Performance Review.* Austin: Office of The Comptroller of Public Accounts.

Sharp, John R. 1992. *Dallas ISD: Performance Review.* Austin: MGT of America.

Sharp, John. 1993. "Introducing the Texas 100." *Fiscal Notes.* October. pp. 10-11.

Simon, Janice. 1994. "Most Advanced Jobs Will Need Advanced Training By 2000," *Galveston Daily News.* July 24.

Sizer, Theodore R. 1992. *Horace's School; Redesigning the American High School.* Boston: Houghton Mifflin Company.

Smothers, Ronald. 1994. "To Raise the Performance of Minorities, a College Increases Its Standards." *The New York Times.* June 29. p. A 11.

Still, Rae Files. 1950. *The Gilmer-Aikin Bills: A Study in the Legislative Process.* Austin, TX: The Steck Company.

Task Force on Education for Economic Growth. 1983. *Action for Excellence.* Denver, CO: Education Commission of the States.

Texas Center for Educational Research. 1990. *Crisis in Texas School Funding: The Pieces of the Puzzle.* Austin: Texas Center for Educational Research.

Texas Education Agency. 1994. *Accountability Manual: The 1994–95 Accountability Rating System for Texas Public Schools and School Districts.* Austin: TEA Office of Planning and Evaluation.

Texas Education Agency. 1993. *Snapshot '93: 1992–93 School District Profiles.* Austin: TEA Office of Policy Planning and Evaluation.

Texas Education Agency. 1990. *Texas School Law Bulletin.* New York: West Publishing.

Texas Education Agency. 1990. *Snapshot: 1988–89 School District Profiles.* Austin: TEA Office of Policy Planning and Evaluation.

Texas Education Agency. 1988. *1988–2000 Long-Range Plan for Technology of the Texas State Board of Education.* Austin: Texas Education Agency.

Texas Elementary Principals and Supervisors Association. 1994. "Accountability Ratings for 1994." *TEPSA Newsletter.* August. p. 6.

Texas Higher Education Coordinating Board. 1994. *Third Annual Report on the Effectiveness of Remediation.* Austin, Texas Higher Education Coordinating Board, Universities and Health Affairs Division.

Texas Public Policy Foundation and National Center for Policy Analysis. 1990. *Choice in Education: Opportunities for Texas.*

Texas Public Policy Foundation and National Center for Policy Analysis. 1990. *Efficiency and Inefficiency in the Texas Public Schools.*

Texas Research League. 1994. *Benchmarks: 1993–94 School District Budgets in Texas.* Austin: Texas Research League.

Texas Research League. 1984. *Texas Public Education: A Matter of Priorities.* Austin: Texas Research League.

Toch, Thomas. 1991. *In the Name of Excellence: The Struggle to Reform the Nations' Schools; Why It's Failing, and What Should Be Done.* New York: Oxford University Press.

United States Bureau of the Census. *Statistical Abstract of the United States: 1992.* (112th edition) Washington, D. C. 1992.

Ward, Pamela. 1994. "Stealing, 'Disobedience' Were Top Youth Crimes in 1973". *Dallas Morning News.* October 6.

Winick, Darwin M. 1991. "Can Business Save Public Education?" Unpublished Speech. Fort Worth, Texas. June 17.

Wolfe, Michael. 1992. *Where We Stand: Can America Make It in The Global Race for Wealth and Happiness?* New York: Bantam.

Yudof, Mark G., David L. Kirp, and Betsy Levin. 1992. *Educational Policy and the Law.* New York: West Publishing.

INDEX

Note: **Boldface** page numbers refer to charts, figures, and tables.

A
Academic performance
    accountability rating standards, **143,** 153
    compensation of teachers and, 78–81
    by minorities, 61–62
    report cards for schools, 65–70, 145–53, **146–48**
    rewarding, 73–81
    School Performance Management, 66–67, 126,
        154–62, **155–56, 158–59, 161–62**
    school performance matrix planning form,
        163–64, **164**
    spending and, **101–3,** 101–11
    testing results for Texas students, 13–25, **14**
Accountability
    authority and, 58–60
    rating standards, **143,** 153
ACT, **103, 141, 148**
Advanced Placement incentive program, 74–77,
    75–77
Agencies to be eliminated, transferred, or combined,
    167
Alexander, Lamar, 6
American College Test, **103, 141, 148**
American Educator, 45, 94
American Federation of Teachers, 24–25, 33
Arizona charter schools, 165
Authority, results and, 52–63

B
Behavior in schools, 93–96
Bennett, William, 48
Bilingual education, 72
Bissenger, G.H., 69
Boy Scouts, 88
Businesses, action required of, 125–29

C
California charter schools, 165
Carnegie Corporation, 120
Certification of teachers, 70, 81–83
Changes in classrom, 84–99
Charter schools, 90–92
    by state, **165–66**

Christian Coalition, 50
Civics, performance in, 20
Classroom changes, 84–99
Class time extension, 87
Clinton, Bill, 6, 55
College admission tests, 151. *See also* ACT; SAT
Colleges, courses not required in, **42**
Colorado charter schools, 165
Community involvement, 108
Compensation of teachers, 78–81
Cortes, Ernesto, 10, 11, 116
Course enrollments, **142**
Crime
    education and, 27
    juvenile, 94, **95**
Curriculum
    courses not required in colleges, **42**
    Hirsch approach, 90
    selected high school course enrollments, **142**
Curriculum for Tomorrow, 50

D
Dallas Independent School District, 154–57
Decentralization in schools, 60
Department of Education, 73
Discipline, 93–96
Diversity, education and, 31
Dropouts, **140, 148,** 150–51
Drucker, Peter, 33

E
Eagle Forum, 50
Earnings
    educational level and, 29, **30**
    of teachers, 78–81
East Dallas Community School, 61–62
Edgewood v. Kirby, 105
Education, factors affecting, **36**
Educational Alternatives, Inc., 91
Educational reform in Texas, 5–12, 33–34
Education associations in Texas, 9–10, 139
Ellis County's Advanced Placement incentive
    program, 74–77, **75–77**

Index

Excellence, rewarding, 73–81
Expenditures by schools, 68–69

F
Failure, rewarding, 71–73
Ferguson, Ronald, 78
Finance system, 100–111
Finn, Chester, 19
Flowers, Terry, 60, 61
Forces of Change, 69
Ford, Terry, 61
Freedom, responsibilities of, 31
Friday Night Lights, 69
Funding for schools
    overhauling finance system, 100–111
    reward system and, 71–81

G
Georgia charter schools, 165
Georgia Tech, 45–46
Gilmer–Aiken law, 105
Goals
    national, 144
    setting, 38–51
Goodwin, Doris Kearns, 39
Governors' Education Summit, 43
Grade inflation, 41–42
Guthrie, James, 55

H
Hawaii charter schools, 165
Hirsch, E.D., 90
Hispanics
    population in Texas, 35
    test results for, 17
Homework, 119–20, **120**
Hostos–Lincoln Academy of Science, 45
House Bill 72, 6–9, 11–12, 34, 81, 113–14

I
IBM, 128
Incentive systems, 74
International Assessment of Educational Progress, 23
International education
    academic performance, 23–25
    days spent in school per year, **118**
    time spent on tasks, **121**
Iron Triangle, 9–10, 113

J
Jackson, Rev. Jesse, 46, 123
Japan, education in, 119–20
Jefferson, Thomas, 30

Jobs, educational requirements for, 22, 47
Just for the Kids, 115–17

K
Kansas charter schools, 165
Kennedy, John F., 39
King, Dr. Martin Luther, 99

L
Legal changes in 1980s, **138**
Literacy skills, performance in, 20–21
Lott, Thaddeus S., 62–63

M
Mabel B. Wesley Elementary School, 62
Massachusetts charter schools, 166
Mathematics, performance in, 19–20, **21, 23**
Michigan charter schools, 166
Microsoft, 87
Minnesota charter schools, 166
Minorities
    Georgia Tech program and, 46
    successful academic performance by, 61–62
Morale of teachers, 57–58

N
National Assessment of Education Progress (NAEP),
    19, 101–2, **103**
National Commission on Children, 22, 23
National goals for education, 144
A Nation at Risk, 5
Needs of children, 96–97
New Mexico charter schools, 166
No Ordinary Time, 39

O
OBE, 48–50
Occupations, educational requirements for, 22, 47
Odessa–Permian High School, 69
O'Donnell Foundation of Dallas, 74
Outcome–based education, 48–50

P
Papert, Seymour, 85–86
Parents
    action required of, 121–25
    choice and, 89
    expectations of schools, 169–70
Performance. *See* Academic performance
Policy changes in 1980s, **138**
Political leaders, action required of, 129–32
Principals, 52–63
Private school voucher system, 92–93

Programs to be eliminated, transferred, or combined, 167
PSAT/NMSQT results, **141**

R
Reich, Robert, 69
Religion in schools, 98–99
Report cards for schools, 65–70, 145–53, **146–48**
Responsibilities of freedom, 31
Results
  authority and, 52–63
  desirable, deciding on, 38–51
  measuring and rewarding, 64–83
Rewards
  for excellence, 73–81
  for failure, 71–73
Riley, Richard, 6
Robertson, Pat, 50
Roosevelt, Franklin D., 38, 39, 87

S
St. Philip's, 60–61
Salaries
  educational level and, 29, **30**
  for teachers, 78–81
Salesmanship Club, 91
SAT, 18, 34, **76, 101–3, 141, 148**
Schlafly, Phyllis, 50
Schneider, Barbara, 121–22
Scholastic Aptitude Test, 18, 34, **76, 101–3, 141, 148**
School districts, breaking up, 89
School Performance Management, 66–67, 126, 154–62, **155–56, 158–59, 161–62**
Schools
  action for, 26–37, 112–32
  downsizing, 89–90
  factors affecting, **36**
  testing results and campus ratings, 13–17
  unfinished reform, 5–12
School year/time extension, 87
Science, performance in, **24**
Shanker, Albert, 11, 25, 33, 48, 74, 88
Sharp, John, 69
Site-based management, 52–54
Skills for jobs, 47
Social services, 96–97
Special education, 72–73
Students, action required of, 117–21
Study rules, 168

T
TAAS, 13–17, 29, 70–71, 146, **146–47,** 150
Taxes, 29, 100–101, 106, 109–10
TBEC, 124, 127
TEA, 9, 15
Teachers
  certification, 70, 81–83
  morale, 57–58
  performance, 67
  salaries, 78–81
Testing. *See also specific tests*
  quality and quantity, 70–71
  results for Texas students, 13–25, **14**
Texas
  academic performance vs. other states, 18
  recent reform efforts in, 6–8
Texas Academic Skills Program, 17
Texas Assessment of Academic Skills, 13–17, 29, 70–71, 146, **146–47,** 150
Texas Business and Education Coalition, 124, 127
Texas Constitution, 105
Texas Education Agency, 9, 15
Texas Elementary Principles and Supervisors Association, 10–11
Texas Federation of Teachers, 11, 95
  survey of student behavior, 93–94, **93**
Texas Legislature, 9
Texas Research League, 100
  survey of businesses, 21–22
Texas Scholars program, 48
Texas Supreme Court, 106
Thurow, Lester, 119

U
Unemployment, educational attainment and, **28**
U.S. Census Bureau, earnings by educational level, 29

V
Violence in schools, 93, 94–95, 96
Virtues, 98–99
Vocational education, 72
Voucher system, 92–93

W
Wages, educational level and, 29, **30**
Wesley Elementary School, 62
Where We Stand, 119
Wisconsin charter schools, 166